I was praying it would all work out, but it didn't look good...

There was a fleeting moment when I thought that maybe, just maybe, they'd give me a chance and it would all work out. Looking into the jurors' eyes, I could see they didn't want to send me to prison.

But then the DA had his turn and everything turned upside down.

He went on and on about all the things I had done. It was horrible, hearing everything he said. It was all true and I felt like sinking through the floor.

When the DA was done, the judge gave the jury very strict instructions. They had to go back into the jury room and decide what to do based *solely* on the law, not their feelings. That took away any shot I had for any sort of second chance. The law was the law. There was no way around it, I was going to jail.

I had quite an entourage in the hallway of the Berks County Courthouse. There were thirty or so people there for me, all waiting for the verdict. My Aunt Martha prayed along with my support group and all my friends. I still get goose bumps when I think of how much all those people loved and supported me.

When the bailiff came out and informed us that the jury was back, I almost lost the contents of my stomach. I walked into the courtroom and not a single juror looked me in the eye. I knew that wasn't a good sign.

Motivational speaker Stacy Butler didn't start out changing people's lives. Far from it. Stacy was a high school head cheerleader, homecoming queen, star athlete, and trendsetter. Her friends and family adored her, and she believed she had it all. Then, out of curiosity, she began flirting with alcohol and drugs. The rush of power that came with coke led her into the world of drug dealing and prostitution as a full-fledged, hardcore pimp. But Stacy got caught and sent to prison, where she learned the hard way that you can't give up if you want to survive.

Her only option was to move forward. That is the ultimate message of *THEY CALLED ME QUEEN B*. The only way out is through, and broken dreams are no excuse for giving up. Sometimes humorous, sometimes brash, always inspirational, Stacy Butler is a courageous voice for survival.

KUDOS for *They Called Me Queen B*

They Called Me Queen B by Stacy Butler is the true story of a young woman from a good family who made a number of bad choices and screwed up her life in a big way. She wasn't a bad person but she got involved with the wrong people, started using and selling drugs, and eventually ended up pimping. When her lifestyle finally caught up with her, Butler was a drug addict along with everything else. Still when it came time to face the music, she did. She got herself into a rehab program, eventually stood trial, and went to prison. Through it all, she showed a rare courage in taking responsibility for her own actions without trying to lay the blame on others. The story was moving, inspiring, and well written. – *Taylor Jones, Reviewer*

They Called Me Queen B by Stacy Butler is a hard-hitting, no holds-barred expose of her life as a drug-dealer and addict. She is caught in a sting/raid by one of her customers who was, in reality, a state trooper. The trooper wants Butler to turn snitch and help build cases against her friends and customers. Butler is no fool, however, and knows very well that her credibility on the street is toast since the raid on her home would now be common knowledge. But she doesn't want to lose her son or end up in jail. So she does the only thing she can, she disappears. However, eventually she realizes she can no longer evade the law and turns herself in. But by now Butler is pregnant and decides it is time to face the consequences of her actions. She is clean and sober by this time and determined to remain so. She also knows life is not going to be easy for some time to come. *They Called Me Queen B* is a touching, inspiring, and thought provoking tale of a courageous young woman who was able to turn her life completely around through faith, guts, and determination. Anyone who has ever used drugs, or who has ever thought about it, should read this book. – *Regan Murphy, Reviewer*

ACKNOWLEDGEMENTS

To my daddy Elfred and the entire Donadson family, my loving husband Jeremy Stripling, my mother-in law momma Ruthie, my second-chance cheerleader Effie Clauser and family, my beautiful children Cain and Melissa, my mentors John Pselus and Ruth Hartman who kept me strong.

To my sister, Michelle, you are in my thoughts lovingly every day. To all the women incarcerated who taught me what true struggle is. My Charcoal Chef family and to the staff and customers of the Silo and Riveredge, *The Reading Eagle* for the opportunity to tell my story, Berks Counseling Center for a place to call home, and all the Friends of Bill who have touched my spirit.

The friends of yesterday, and today, you are all part of my story, and you know who you all are.

They Called Me Queen B

Stacy Butler

A Black Opal Books Publication

GENRE: NON-FICTION/MEMOIRS/INSPIRATIONAL

This book is a work of non-fiction. All information and opinions expressed herein are the views of the author. This publication is intended to provide accurate and authoritative information concerning the subject matter covered and is for informational purposes only. Neither the author nor the publisher is attempting to provide legal advice of any kind. All trademarks, service marks, registered trademarks, and registered service marks are the property of their respective owners and are used herein for identification purposes only. The publisher does not have any control over or assume any responsibility for author or third-party websites or their contents.

THEY CALLED ME QUEEN B
Copyright © 2014 by Stacy Butler Stripling
Cover Design by Jackson Cover Designs
All cover art copyright © 2014
All Rights Reserved
Print ISBN: 978-1-626941-15-1

First Publication: MARCH 2014

All rights reserved under the International and Pan-American Copyright Conventions. No part of this book may be reproduced or transmitted in any form or by any means, electronic or mechanical, including photocopying, recording, or by any information storage and retrieval system, without permission in writing from the publisher.

WARNING: The unauthorized reproduction or distribution of this copyrighted work is illegal. Criminal copyright infringement, including infringement without monetary gain, is investigated by the FBI and is punishable by up to 5 years in federal prison and a fine of $250,000.

ABOUT THE PRINT VERSION: If you purchased a print version of this book without a cover, you should be aware that the book is stolen property. It was reported as "unsold and destroyed" to the publisher, and neither the author nor the publisher has received any payment for this "stripped book."

IF YOU FIND A PRINT VERSION OF THIS BOOK BEING SOLD OR SHARED ILLEGALLY, PLEASE REPORT IT TO: lpn@blackopalbooks.com.

Published by Black Opal Books: **http://www.blackopalbooks.com**

DEDICATION

This book is dedicated to Melissa Butler.

You are my everything. The hardest worker and caregiver I have ever known. May you rest in peace in glory with your father forever. I love you mother, the truest queen.

CHAPTER 1

It was a random Sunday in Reading, Pennsylvania. I just wanted to get high and not move. I didn't care about much else back then.

I just wanted to get high.

Five people were chilling at my house that day, all with the same goal. That's how it was at my place. My two-story row house had three bedrooms and one bathroom. It was my mother's first FHA home, and I'd turned it into a crack house.

There were no doors inside. One room just led to another. No privacy, either, but no one cared. It was a place to go where you could stay, do drugs, and be left alone—a place where some would come and squat. People just liked it there.

Every drug addict was different and I dealt with ones on every level. Scared and from the city, some bought fifty dollars' worth of coke from me, then rolled out, never staying. Others shelled out five hundred bucks or more. The ones from the suburbs had to be handled with kid gloves. My job was to make them feel safe. It was a job I did well. I was a rarity in my hometown, a bi-racial overachiever, even as an addict.

Sherry, one of my best customers, had come through on Friday, bringing a thousand in cash. She and I had been up for two days smoking crack. It was the best. The girl had nowhere to go, no one else she trusted. Imagine that. She'd come in and we'd get high together.

When a customer bought from me, that person usually would "break off" the house, meaning they would give me some and we'd get high together. After all, anybody who came through knew the risks involved for both of us. Most couldn't go home to families, so they'd chill with me, knowing they were safe. No one would come looking for them, because I had thugs there, whose job it was to make sure no one who wasn't welcome got in. No one minded breaking off to me. It was just what they did.

So I had been high for two days straight and didn't have to spend a dime. Besides, I liked Sherry, kind of the way I liked Tonya. Tonya was a single-mom, home-health aide, who came around from time to time.

Sherry never actually smoked. She sniffed. I smoked. I got a whole bunch of powdered cocaine and cooked it up myself, with water and baking soda, which made it even better. When you bought crack on the street, it was mixed with a whole bunch of shit you didn't want. But if I cooked it, I trusted it, and I knew it was good.

So I'd smoke and Sherry would sniff, and everyone else would buy from me, even though she'd bought the whole thing we were sharing. I'd always make money from every angle, as many ways as I could.

To take a hit, I'd light up the crack pipe, which was a straight glass pipe with no bowl at the end. It had a screen that I'd put the crack rock on. I'd fill it as much as I could. Most people just put in something like twenty dollars' worth, but I had so much crack there that day that I put in something like a hundred bucks' worth.

When I smoked that much crack, I wasn't interested in sitting around. Most people wanted to just veg out. Not me. I liked to move, to go shopping and shit like that. Man, sometimes I'd clean the house. That day, I wanted to do laundry. It was something with action.

I knew Sherry had a truck, so I rounded up all my dirty clothes and stuffed them in her little midget pickup. Right before I left, I took a big blast from the crack pipe, a hundred-dollar hit, and was so high it was unreal. We'd call that a mega blast when it was that huge. Man, I was so high, my ears actually rang.

Once I took that hit, I was all set for the laundromat. But I realized I'd be at the laundromat for a while and wanted to keep the high going, so I grabbed some beer, stuffed another C-note of crack in my wallet, and headed out.

I'd just gotten into the truck when I heard a loud thumping on my window. It scared the shit out of me. When I turned, I saw a badge plastered to the window.

Fuck!

I think my heart stopped beating for a minute.

Shit!

I finally focused on the person holding the badge. She was a heavyset cop wearing a black T-shirt and jeans, her brown hair pulled back in a ponytail.

"Stacy, open the door." Her voice penetrated my fog.

That voice! I know that voice.

Suddenly, it hit me. I recognized her face and voice at the same time.

No way! It couldn't be. Not Tonya.

I looked up into the eyes of the trooper. "Fuck!" I opened the door. "I knew it. I knew it."

"Should have gone with your gut, Stacy." Her voice was calm. "Get into my car, right now."

I couldn't move. "Fuck."

"Don't make a scene," she said. "Just get in and be quiet. Everything's going to be okay if you listen to me. Got it?"

Keeping my mouth shut, I let her guide me into the back seat of the white Chevy, the trademark unmarked cop car for Reading. She climbed in beside me, sitting back there while her partner drove around the block. She stared at me while I looked out the window, trying to make sense of what was happening.

This state trooper, Tonya, was someone I'd done three drug sales with. My head was spinning.

What the fuck is going on?

Tonya was a single mom living in Birdsboro, who needed extra money. She was fighting an ugly custody battle for her two kids. She was trying to keep her kids and needed the money. It was a cause I could get behind.

This soccer-mom drug dealer from the suburbs seemed classy to me, a business woman. I didn't know too many people like her. I'd give her a good price for the coke, and she'd resell to her rich friends and make a bundle. It was what she needed to do to get her kids back from her ex.

She'd come to the house, bringing Yuengling beer, the good stuff, which we'd drink together. She never smoked, but that was fine. I'm not the type to push. It's not good business. If someone didn't want to smoke, it wasn't a problem. She was buying from me, and that's all I cared about, because that meant I'd make money and get high that night.

Our first transaction was small. I got it from some kid on the street. The next time was a bit bigger. Again, I found another kid to sell to me. Then she came one day with a shitload of cash. We did a real big deal together, fourteen grams of cocaine.

I was "cash only" on the street for the same reason most addict dealers were. I'd lost my connections because if anyone gave me crack, I'd use rather than sell.

No one trusted me anymore, with good reason. When I was starting out, I'd had big connections who would give me coke on consignment. I wouldn't have to pay for it until the customer paid me. But I no longer had that kind of clout.

A friend of mine, who didn't use himself, had the connections I lacked and he could get his hands on big amounts. He told me to meet him at a bar in West Reading, so I took Tonya there, did the deal, and left.

That big deal had gone down a week ago. A couple days later, I had gotten the call that my friend, who'd set up the deal, was in jail.

"What happened?"

"He got busted by the cops the night you were with him. Stacy, you should stop what you're doing."

"Yeah, well, I'll think about it."

Sure, I felt bad that my friend had been used as a pawn. I felt even worse that I had played a part in his arrest. But I couldn't stop what I was doing. Besides, the bust might have gone down anyway. The cops could have been watching him or his big connection.

All I could think about was getting high.

I had missed all the warning signals about Tonya.

No, that's not what happened, not if I'm being honest. I didn't miss the signs, I ignored them. Maybe it was because, as surrounded as I was by people, I was lonely, and she was good company. Maybe part of the reason was that my son, Cain, meant the world to me, even back then, and she seemed to understand what I was going through when we talked about our kids. After all, she was a home health aide at Manor Care, so I took comfort in talking to someone about dealing with my eleven year old son with Asperger's Syndrome.

The truth was, although I related to her as a single mom and I liked the idea of helping her get her kids back from her ex, my biggest motivation was that I wanted to get high. Tonya's visits meant that I could, so I ignored the obvious signals that she wasn't who she said she was.

When this soccer mom came in with her pockets full of money for that last deal, my eyes lit up.

"Well, obviously you can see that I'm not exactly who I told you I was," Tonya said, her words penetrating the deep fog that was surrounding me, snapping me back to the moment.

I stared at her. Shock and drugs don't mix well, and that day, Tonya showing up in her trooper gear was one of those times. I stared at the badge on a chain around her neck. It was beyond weird. Each time I had seen her before, she'd been in scrubs. The picture didn't match.

"So you're not a nurse then?" I asked slowly.

She coughed to cover her laugh. "No, I'm not a nurse." Then she paused and her eyes softened a bit. She looked like the old Tonya again. "Stacy, I'm a state trooper."

"Yeah, I can see that."

"Look, I'm not going to arrest you," she said. "That's why I put you in the car and I'm driving around with you. I don't normally do that when I bust someone."

Thank God! All the tension went out of my body. I sank back into the seat. I wasn't going to jail. The relief was incredible. Then it hit me.

Wait, what?

I sprang back up. "Why? Why aren't you going to arrest me?"

She gave me a soft smile. "We have something to offer you."

"Like what?"

"We want you to work for us, give us information. We're confident that you can help us big time."

I knew enough to say what she wanted to hear, regardless of anything. Without hesitation, I replied, "I'll do whatever you want me to do."

She laughed. "I thought you might feel that way."

"Tonya, right now, I just need to get out of this car and go home," I said. I couldn't keep the whine out of my voice.

I need to get high now! My mind screamed out at me painfully. The wonderful mega blast I'd taken moments before had worn off pretty much the instant I saw the shine of her badge.

She looked at me and sighed. "Sam," she said to her partner, "head back to Stacy's house."

The driver nodded and made a left turn. We were two minutes from my house. Tonya understood me, knew what I needed without my saying the words. Maybe she was still my friend.

"Thank you," I whispered.

"Here's my card." Her voice was soft and soothing. "Call me in the morning, when you wake up, okay?"

I nodded. "Sure thing."

When we pulled up to my house, I reached for the door handle. She grabbed my shoulder. "Go on in and act as if I never picked you up," she said, her voice stern. "Don't you dare tell anyone who I am, got it? You just keep going on doing what you're doing."

I looked at her and knew she meant every word she said. I gulped and got out of the car, heading for the back door.

Great. Now I've got to pretend like I'm just like everyone else when I'm not.

How the fuck was I supposed to pull that off? It wasn't like everyone hadn't just seen me get picked up in a cop car or anything. What the hell was I supposed to do now?

My feet felt like lead as I stumbled to the back door. I walked in and was immediately greeted by my crackhead house guests, with a frenzied, "What happened?"

And then:

"You okay?"

"Where did you go?"

"What's going on?"

"Shit, a friend of mine just played a prank on me." My laugh sounded forced and high-pitched, even to my ears. "She's a real clown. Picked me up in a cop car and drove me around, totally killed my high!"

Looking around, I could tell I'd pulled it off, for a while at least. No one seemed to care. Everyone went back to what they were doing.

Me? Well, at that moment I just needed to try not to think about what tomorrow would bring. I just needed to lose myself in a good hundred-dollar high.

CHAPTER 2

Things were chill for a few hours. With every hit from the crack pipe, I got more and more paranoid.

Shit, what am I going to do?

My whole world had just turned upside down and no one seemed to notice. No one cared. People around me weren't interested.

I jumped when someone knocked on the door. Opening it, I saw it was some guy from across the street.

"What happened? I saw a cop."

"It was a joke, that's all." It was starting to sound incredibly lame to my ears.

"Some joke," he muttered.

"What do you mean by that?" I said.

The asshole doesn't believe me. Though, I didn't think everyone in the house was really buying my story either. Everything would fall apart if they didn't believe me. I had to be a convincing liar. Man, if word got out that I was with the cops, I could get killed.

Fuck, there goes my high again!

I couldn't stay high. The adrenaline kept coming in, killing it. Pissed as hell, I kicked people out of my house. I needed to call my mother, tell her what happened, but I couldn't do that with a house full of crack heads.

It was seven in the morning before everyone was gone. It had taken me twelve hours to clear the house. We had so much cocaine but I couldn't keep a high.

Finally, I was clean out of drugs, beer, and even cigarettes. I was jonesing like mad, dying. I was so desperate that I smoked butts out of an ashtray. I kept thinking about how I was going to go to jail and lose my kid.

Everything just came crashing down around me all of a sudden. I think that was probably when I reached my bottom, that place so low you can't go lower.

I flopped back onto the couch. For the first time, I noticed how disgusting it was, with dirty brown stains and springs popping out all over. My hand rested against a stain that looked like it had been there for months. Pizza sauce?

Why haven't I seen that fucking gross stain before?

I looked around the house like I'd never seen any of it before. It was a gigantic mess. Everything looked out of place and weird.

It occurred to me that maybe there was something more important than where the next high was coming from. I was actually living in filth. Maybe this was what having a conscience felt like.

There was one person I needed to talk to. She'd find out soon enough, but I wanted to be the one to tell her. I picked up the phone and called my mother.

"They finally busted me," I said as soon as she picked up.

"Stacy?" Her voice was groggy. "What are you talking about?"

I gave her a rundown on the events from last night. It came out as a jumbled slur of words. I told her about Tonya, about the deal they offered. I told her everything.

She was silent as she listened to my rambling. Finally, she said, "You stupid bitch," then hung up.

My mom had known what I was doing, but I always felt like I had to tell her. She was my mom. I just didn't want to have any secrets from her, ever. My attitude always sucked, though, and I knew it, even high. If she didn't like something I did, I'd tell her that I didn't give a shit. I didn't. If she didn't like the house the way I kept it, I'd tell her not to visit. That's how I was. Not exactly the model daughter.

As I held the beeping phone receiver in my hand, tears streamed down my face. All that disrespectful stuff I'd said to her was really more the crack talking than me. I actually really *did* care what she thought.

I wonder if she knows that.

It was tough growing up with a white mom and black dad. In the 1970s, that wasn't an easy thing. It's not particularly easy any time, but during that period, the Klan was alive and well in Reading, Pennsylvania. That meant my parents couldn't be seen walking down the street together. It was too dangerous.

Mom got kicked out of her house when she got pregnant with me. Her parents wanted nothing to do with her, so she had to live with friends and sleep on their floor. She wound up in the projects. She was a survivor though, wanting to make the best of things, so she enrolled in beauty school to become a cosmetologist. She wasn't going down without a fight.

When Mom gave birth to me, her mother showed up. Mom said Grandmother fell in love with me immediately. But Granddad never could get over the disgrace of his little girl getting knocked up by a black man. He figured his precious blood line had been tainted or something. Well, that ended my grandparents' marriage. Grandma wanted to see her grandbaby and that was that.

I never met my biological maternal grandfather. Never cared to, really.

Grandma later married a man who lived across the street. He was the best friend of her son, my Uncle Barry. He was a good twenty years younger than my grandmother, so there our family was again with that familiar cloud of controversy hanging over us.

My new granddad loved me and I loved him. I'd call him Pappy and thought of him as my real grandfather. He and my grandmother really raised me, because Mom had to work a lot. Pappy was German Dutch, so I had a classic Dutch upbringing.

Being black, looking black, and living in a white neighborhood sucked big time. To say that Pappy's family didn't like me much was a gross understatement. When his family had a festive dinner, like Thanksgiving, Nanny and Pappy had to leave me behind. They'd go across the street for the family celebration, while I stayed home by myself.

When Uncle Barry got married, he married a white girl, so the family was in love with her. She was literally the girl next door. They had a big wedding that everyone attended, including my mother. Well, everyone but me. I tried not to let it bother me, but it did.

I knew that my mom and grandparents loved me and that pretty much made up for things. Mom went out of her way to make sure I was around both whites and blacks, experiencing both cultures. I went to Southwest Junior High, which was on the other side of town. Northeast Junior High was all white. But it was cool, because I knew the kids from Northeast and got to know the ones from Southwest, too.

Before long, Mom got her beautician's license, but didn't like the work that much. She decided to go to nursing school and become an RN. The crazy thing was that she broke her leg, so she never actually finished nursing school, but she stayed in the field. She worked as a nursing assistant at a hospital for elderly people. She worked third shift, so I didn't see her much.

My mother was one to keep working hard to better herself. She took the civil service test, so that she could work for Wernersville State Hospital. She still worked third shift, but made much better money. Coincidentally, my father worked at Wernersville, too. They worked side by side for twenty-five years.

Mom and Dad stayed friends. To his credit, my father always took care of us financially, making sure we had what we needed. He hustled drugs on the side, marijuana mostly, but never got caught.

My mom only had sex with two men in her entire life. The second guy, Carl, was always good to me. He was a drug addict, so not much help, though. I called him "Cuddy." He was always drunk and high, but affectionate.

I always admired my mom's smarts and ability. She made decent money, saved it, and spent it on things she wanted. For one thing, she always had decent cars. Her favorites, an Audi and a Caddie, were now mine.

She worked hard, got an FHA loan, and moved out of the projects. She was so proud when she finally bought her place. She did it all by herself, no help from anyone. That was my mom. So I understood why she hung up on me and called me a stupid bitch. Honestly, I didn't blame her.

I took out the trooper's card. I stared at it for a moment and realized that there was no turning back. My life was going to be different. No getting around that. I was still crying when I dialed her number.

"Tonya, I really need for you to come over here," I said.

"I'll be there within an hour," she said.

Thank God.

True to her word, within an hour she was sitting on my filthy sofa, in jeans and a T-shirt with some slogan on it. I stared at her. She looked so different from what I remembered.

"You okay?" she asked.

"No," I said. Fresh tears poured out. "Everything is upside down."

"Stacy, you've got a choice. You can come work for me or you can go to jail for a very, very long time."

"I don't know what to do," I said.

Tonya was still my friend and I knew she'd give me good advice. I trusted her to look out for me and help me to do the right thing.

"We have enough evidence on you, enough proof, and enough cocaine, to lock you up for at least five to ten years." Her voice was hard.

Friends don't lock each other away!

My world started spinning on me. I started crying hysterically. "Oh my God! Oh my God!"

She allowed me to continue for a while, waiting for me to calm down a bit. She then dropped a bomb on me. "We've been watching you for some time," she said. "We know everyone that comes and goes."

She pulled out pictures—friends coming in and out, clients. And there was my mom, bringing Cain home one day.

"Shit, you have pictures of my mom and Cain?" I cried.

"We have everyone." Her voice was calm and patient.

It was all a little too real. The pictures brought everything home. Tonya wasn't lying. They had everything on me. They knew everything.

"Who took these pictures?" I asked, trying to wrap my wits around everything, which was spinning out of control.

"Our photographer, George Walken," she said.

"No way," I whispered. I knew that guy, from high school of all things. We'd graduated together, for God's sake. So now a fellow student, a classmate, was watching me? Taking pictures for the cops? For some reason, that made everything much worse. It was just too real.

"I'm a good person," I said. "You just don't know who I am. You don't know what I've been through. You just don't know."

"But I do know. People don't smoke crack for shits and giggles." She paused and let that sink in a little. "People smoke crack because there are major problems in their lives. Real shit. I know. Crack's no joke, Stacy. It's a serious mental obsession. You don't just do that because everything's fine in your life. You and I've talked about some of your problems. I know."

So while I had been pouring my soul out to her, she'd been taking notes, trying to figure out how to use that shit against me. She didn't give a fuck about me. She was lying about everything. Everything!

It suddenly hit me. Who was this bitch? "Do you even have kids?"

She laughed at me. "No, I don't have children."

"What's so funny about that?"

She looked like she was debating whether to tell me. Finally, she said, "It's just that the boys down at the precinct thought that was a funny gag. I mean, I'm the least likely person to have a child, if you know what I mean."

I looked at her for a moment or two. What the hell did she mean? Then it hit me. Fuck, she was gay! I'd thought so. When I first met her, I thought, *This fucking chick is gay*! There was just something about her. Again, I'd caught the signals, but I hadn't cared. I just wanted to get high. And she was my ticket.

"And Karin?" I asked. It was hitting me like some fucking downpour of knowledge. "Is Karin really your niece?"

"How do you think we found you, anyway?" She let that sink in.

Karin had been one of my strippers. She had vouched for Tonya, so I figured she was okay. Karin said she was her aunt. Shit, the bitch played me.

Still, I had to admit that after the first sale, I did some digging around. I checked Tonya's story out a bit. There was just something off, something not quite right.

I knew a nurse who worked at Manor Care, so I asked her about Tonya. She didn't know anyone by that name. I mean, I knew that was weird, but I'd just ignored it, figured there was some reason for it. Maybe Tonya had a good reason to lie. And what the fuck did it matter, anyway? I'd let my desire to get wasted outweigh every bit of instinct I had.

"So, she's not…you're not her aunt then."

"No, Karin's what we call a confidential informant, someone who gets paid to turn people in," Tonya said.

"I know what a CI is," I said through gritted teeth. "It's a fucking snitch."

"Yeah, and she did her job with you," she said. "Now you're going to lead us to the big-time drug dealers. That's what's going to keep you out of jail."

"Stacy the snitch," I mumbled. "Doesn't sound like me."

"How about Stacy the convict? Does that sound better?"

"No!" I said, glaring at her.

I couldn't see myself willingly going to jail, not if I had any other option. I continued to stare at her, thinking about how my life had become a train wreck, when suddenly the front door crashed open. Within seconds, my small living room was filled with men in uniforms.

Loud, demanding voices called out, "COBRA police, everyone on the floor!"

They didn't need to repeat themselves. Tonya and I were both flat on our stomachs on the floor within seconds. My heart was pounding in my chest. Shit! It was nine in the morning and just when I was trying to get a handle on my life, my house was raided. Why was Tonya next to me on the floor? Did I lose my chance to be a CI?

What the fuck is going on?

CHAPTER 3

COBRA was a special city police task force in Reading, focused on drug trafficking. They raided homes like mine, known drug dens. Apparently, they'd been watching me, but failed to talk to the state police, so they didn't have a clue what Tonya's team was doing there.

Tonya's voice cut through the chaos that had burst through the front door. "Look in my back pocket! Look who I am!" she shouted.

Please don't shoot me! I plead silently.

About fifteen cops had their guns trained on us as we lay on the floor. One of them moved toward Tonya. My cheek still pressed against my dirty carpet, I watched him carefully as he pulled out Tonya's badge and credentials. His face fell like a cartoon character. Under different circumstances it might have been funny.

"Uh, oh," he said, looking apologetically at her. "I'm sorry, Officer."

He signaled to the others in the room to lower their weapons. "She's state."

Tonya stood up slowly and grabbed her badge from him. She was pissed. "This is *my* investigation!"

Both state and city had pretty big egos, but in this case, state trumped city and city had to go. Tonya was furious and everyone in the room knew it. They'd crossed a line and they were going to catch shit for it. The city cops all put their guns away.

"What the fuck do you think you're doing? If you've fucked up my investigation in any way, you're all losing your badges. What the hell were you thinking? What sort of fucked up operation is this?" Tonya was screaming at the top of her lungs by now. "Get the hell out of here before you do any more damage."

"We didn't know," the lead guy said. A moment ago, he looked all tough, but now he had the look of a frightened child.

"And that's my problem, how?"

"I'm just saying, we were told to bust this crack house."

Tonya glared at him. "Get this straight, motherfucker. This girl has a pass."

I looked at the man and then at Tonya. Did she just tell these cops that I had a pass? As I looked around at them, it hit me.

I have a green light.

I was being given permission to do whatever the fuck I wanted to do, whenever I wanted to do it. I could smoke crack any time I wanted to and no one could do anything. I was above the law. Shit, I could go through red lights and nobody could pull me over. They'd be interfering with my drug deal. Sort of like some deputy with immunity or something. If someone dared to stop me from doing a drug deal, they'd catch shit for it. Fuck, I was more powerful than ever.

Tonya called it in and the COBRA men all got reprimanded. Then they left. I waved at them cheerfully as they filed out of my home. I mean shit, they couldn't touch me. I didn't have to worry about anything. I'd just been elevated into a new realm of importance. It was like I'd just been given membership into some exclusive country club for crack heads.

The only problem was there was so much attention drawn to my house, because of them busting in like that, I'd lose any remaining credibility with my clientele. I mean if they had arrested me, dragged me out of the house, in cuffs, that might have played on the street better. Tonya should have thought of that. She should have put me in handcuffs for show, but she didn't.

Fifteen cops broke into my home and then just walked away, letting me go back to smoking crack there that night. What other explanation could there be? The people around me were pretty out of it, but they weren't stupid. They'd know something was up.

"People are going to know I'm a snitch," I muttered as the last of the COBRA unit drove off.

"It doesn't look good," Tonya said.

"What are you doing to do?"

"I'll pick you up in the morning and we'll go over what you'll need to do. We'll make this work and we'll protect you."

I nodded my head. I mean, like, what choice did I have, anyway? It was this or going to jail for a real long time. Becoming a CI seemed like the right decision. I just wasn't coming to terms with it so well. My doubts must have shown on my face.

"Think of Cain, Stacy," Tonya said. She sounded like the old Tonya, the one that used to sit on my couch talking about her kids while I got high. "What's going to happen to him if you're in jail?"

"I have no idea."

"You think your mom can handle him?"

"No," I said, feeling like my world was caving in.

"Your sister?"

"I don't know."

She touched my shoulder. "You really want him to wind up in foster care?"

I shook my head. "Okay, I'll do it."

Tonya smiled. "Good. It's the right thing to do."

She took off and I collapsed back onto the couch. What was going to happen to Cain? His Asperger's was no joke. Asperger's was the highest functioning level on the autistic spectrum. What would happen to him if I left?

I had met Cain's father, Jessie, a gorgeous Hispanic athletic type, back in high school. It was much more than a crush. I was in love. I think I fell for him when I first saw him on the baseball field. He really filled out that uniform. He made me so hot, I just had to have him.

When he graduated from high school, he turned into a drug addict and crack head. It was a pretty sudden transformation. I didn't care, though. I was obsessed with the man, so I hooked up with him. Then I found out I was pregnant a month after we had sex. Shit, talk about bad luck.

I had gestational diabetes when I was pregnant. Jessie was so bad off that he would steal my needles and sell them on the street. I was pretty naïve back then, not realizing how bad his obsession was. I had no clue about bad crack addictions. I sniffed coke and thought it was pretty much the same thing. I didn't know that crack was much worse. It didn't take me long to figure it out though.

Jessie went spiraling downhill fast. Not surprising. He went from being a charming kid in a baseball uniform to a mean crack head who was high all the time. It wasn't long before he started beating me, wailing on me mercilessly. My pregnant belly didn't stop him. He didn't need a reason. He just wanted to get his anger out.

One time, we were arguing in the street about something. He was pissed and started beating me, not caring that we were in public. My sister, Megan, was there. She went into shock, screaming as I lay in the street bleeding.

"You fucking cunt whore!" he shouted as he pummeled me.

Wham! I saw a flash, as he hit my head. Wham! Another.

"Please, Jessie," I cried out.

Wham! Another flash. I think I counted fifteen flashes within a space of three minutes.

When Jessie left, Megan collapsed next to me. I remember the smell of urine on her.

"Why don't you leave him?" she asked me later.

"I can change him," I said. I think I believed it, too.

There was one time when I was holding Cain and he beat me until I dropped my baby. Even then I didn't leave Jessie. He was my drug and I was hooked.

He never worked, so I worked three jobs while Jessie smoked crack. He would even steal Cain's formula, selling it for more money.

It wasn't until Cain was almost two years old that I noticed something was wrong with him. My friend's daughter, who was about three days older than him, was singing in the background while I was on the phone with my friend. Cain couldn't even talk. That scared me.

Since my mom was a trained nurse, I confided my concerns to her.

"Don't worry so much," she said.
"I think he should be talking by now."
"Boys are slow. He's not even two."
"I don't know."
"He's fine."
But he's not fine.
I took him to the doctor. I wanted to help him. I was right, he wasn't fine. In the end, I got social security checks because of his illness. It was a steady stream of income, so that I could pay bills. Actually, it was more than I needed for bills, so I got high with the rest.

When Cain turned three, Jessie left me for another woman. It was a blessing. I took up with another guy, who was great with Cain. He and his mom kept my son away from a lot of the shit that was going on.

Trying to be a decent parent, I'd do my best to keep Cain upstairs while I'd smoke crack in the kitchen. I had a curtain separating the kitchen and living room. I'd take food up to him and let him play on his Playstation. He loved that thing, so he'd stay occupied and not come downstairs.

My regulars considered Cain family and they'd hang with him upstairs. When a new game came out, they'd rush over to play it with him. Cain knew all my regulars by name, giving them hugs when they came in. One of his favorites was a girl, Sara, who'd come over with tons of cash. When Cain saw her, he knew it meant one thing. He was going to Walmart to get whatever he wanted.

My friend, Frank, loved Sara, too. She just threw money around. Sara would give him hundreds of dollars to get her drugs. He'd break off to me, giving me my cut. It was a good con. Frank was good at convincing her that she hadn't paid him for something yet, pulling more money from her. Then the dealer who gave Frank the bags of coke would give him extras. I had him so well trained. He'd always break off to me, without my even asking. I could trust him.

My house was a non-stop party. Cain would ask me to "Put on the God music." He loved gospel. So I'd put it on and we'd try to go to sleep, but it didn't last. Before long, someone would wake me up, coming to the door and be like, "Yo, Stacy, I got a lot of shit!" That drug called me, all hours of the day and night.

But now, my life was about to change, radically and permanently. Tonya was right, I didn't have a choice. I had to do what I could to protect my son, and if that meant becoming a CI, that's what I had to do.

The next day, Tonya was there at nine in the morning sharp as promised. She took me over to the police barracks in Kenhorst, where an officer photographed and fingerprinted me, all part of the protocol.

Then she brought me into another room with other cops. They went over their plans for me, telling me how I could set up at a Mexican bar and snitch for them. I listened and nodded. The Mexicans had no idea who I was, so it could work. It wouldn't have worked in my area. I was too well known. I don't want to brag or anything, but I had a name on the street.

They called me Queen B.

I had to admit, I liked it. I got that name from the kingpin of the biggest coke ring in Reading. I met the man when I lived in West Reading back in 2000. Tracing it back, that's when I really started dealing. My drug career really took off there.

That place in West Reading was a three-story townhouse behind a diner. There were two tenants on the bottom, two in the middle and three on the top. I ended up getting every single person in that townhouse high. Everyone was on drugs and they all bought from me. It was all me. It was all the Queen B.

And that's when I became a pimp.

I had all kinds of gang members coming through my townhouse. Bloods, Crypts, Kingpins, Latin Kings, all rival gangs. Since sex was universal, it was okay. They'd give me drugs to get what they wanted, and they kept their cool.

When Karin snitched me out to Tonya, the cops knew they'd hit pay dirt. They saw all the people I was connected to and shit their pants. I had connections out the ass. I knew the whales, the big-time dealers. I could get a hold of a hundred grams of coke in five minutes.

But they didn't seem interested in my higher ups. They wanted me to start over, in the Mexican bar they staked out, and do ten to twelve controlled buys. They knew there were big drugs in there and they wanted me to go after it. They wanted to own a piece of that.

Really, they wanted to own me.

So that day, in the police station, I agreed to be their CI. What was I going to say?

The room of cops relaxed. Tonya smiled at me. "Stacy, just keep doing what you're doing."

I nodded and gave her a weak smile. "I can do that."

"You're doing great," she said. "Stay high and make your connections. It will all work out for everyone. You included."

I was shaking when I left the station. This is the stuff of movies, not real life. Like they're really going to let me go get high and do big drug deals. It had to be some kind of elaborate plan to entrap and arrest me.

The more I thought about it, though, the more I realized that if they wanted to arrest me, they'd have done it already. They had everything they needed to lock me up for a long time. So then, what would be the purpose of all this? I looked behind me, no one following, no guns trained on my back.

That's a good sign.

The whole thing made my head spin. It was too much to think about and my high was wearing off. I'd taken a huge hit before going into the station and now I needed another. I could only hope that things would look better when I was high.

CHAPTER 4

I stumbled to my front door. It was late morning and I was ready to light up and hide from the world. Suddenly, I saw a card from CYS, Child and Youth Services. I reached out to steady myself on the door frame.

Now? Are you fucking shitting me?

I looked around, scanning the neighborhood.

Who told on me?

It was so crazy. God's timing. I'd never had any dealings with CYS. Ever! I mean I should have, what with all that went on in my house. Then it hit me.

Fuck, my urine's hot!

CYS came over and tested my urine later that day. Of course, it tested positive for coke and weed. They agreed not to take Cain away from me immediately. I'd have to go through random urine tests and a bunch of crap that I couldn't deal with.

I called my mom. "You're going to have to pick up Cain."

"Why?" She sounded pissed.

"My urine's hot," I said. "I can't keep him."

"What's your plan?" she asked.

I told her all about my meeting with Tonya and the deal they offered me. When I finished, she was silent.

"Mom?" I asked. "You still there?"

"You're not going to do it, are you?"

"You mean be a CI?" I asked.

"Yes."

"I don't think I can."

She paused for a moment. "So, what are you going to do?"

"Get clean, Mom. I don't have any other choice if I want to keep my son."

Mom's voice cracked. "I'm proud of you."

She picked up Cain an hour later. The house was eerily quiet. When I realized what I was doing, my lungs stopped pumping oxygen. What the hell was I thinking? It was one thing to say that I'd quit crack and another to actually do it, and alcohol, too.

And to make things worse, I missed Cain.

Shit, can I really do this?

I almost changed my mind.

But if I didn't get clean, my urine would always be hot, and it was not like the cops could keep CYS off my back. No, if I didn't make this change, I'd lose Cain forever.

Fuck, the cops are going to freak!

If they found me, I'd be facing serious jail time. Going back as far as I could remember, I always talked shit about women who lost their kids. They always seemed so weak and selfish. I couldn't stomach them and certainly couldn't become one of them, no matter what. Cain was always with me, part of my life.

But even when I was in the PTA, for Christ's sake, I had a crack pipe in my purse.

So now that I realized I'd be reneging on the deal I'd just made with Tonya, all the real-world stuff hit me like a fist in the stomach.

Where the fuck am I going to live?

I couldn't stay at the Birch Street crack house. I'd get caught for sure. In fact, I realized I needed to leave immediately. I'd sneak back in a few days to get some odds and ends, but that thought made my heart feel like it was a wild animal, trying to get out of my chest. The cops would arrest me on the spot if they knew I was there.

The next morning, I went to TASC, the county agency where you go to get a bed for rehab. But there were no beds available! Shit, here I was, making the right decision for the first time in my life and the county was all filled up. I wasn't going to survive long.

I'm going to die.

I was one hundred twenty pounds soaking wet. I used to weigh almost four hundred pounds, but coke killed my appetite for days at a time. It was a horrible diet plan.

When I told my mom I wasn't going back to Birch Street, she put the house up on the market. People squatted there, smoking crack after I was gone, as though I'd never left. She sold it quickly, within thirty days or something, for a loss of fifteen thousand. Thanks to me, her first FHA home was gone.

I ended up staying with the only person I could think of, the John of one of my most obedient prostitutes. I don't remember his name, but he lived on Union Street in a row home like mine, except his was tidy and relatively safe. Only my mom and a few girls knew I was staying there.

Grateful as I was, I knew this John and knew I had to make sure to always have a girl with me, someone he could fuck when he got high on coke. I sure as hell wasn't going to have sex with him.

He let me get high there, too. I couldn't help it. I still craved crack. I wasn't sober yet and was waiting for something to open up so that I could get clean. It was still a better environment for me than Birch Street. I mean, nobody was there all hours of the night, and Cain was safe with my mom.

Sitting in that house, pimping out girls so I could hide away from the cops, in the hope of getting off crack,

I couldn't stop thinking about everything that happened to get me there. It just wasn't what I thought my life would turn into when I was in high school.

Throughout my teen years, I was always in the in-crowd. I was invited to all the cool parties. It wasn't a party if Stacy Butler wasn't there. I was part of the homecoming court clique, head cheerleader to boot. The only thing that wasn't perfect was that I was overweight. Still, it didn't stop me. I didn't let it.

Knowing me now, I bet some people thought I was a weirdo, a recluse maniac who had to withdraw and use drugs and alcohol to escape. I started with drugs because I was a partier. That's what partiers did. It was a social thing.

I started with pot and alcohol. Some people say those two drugs are harmless, but I now see saw them as gateway drugs for young kids, especially alcohol. It's legal and considered acceptable. I hope that pot never becomes legal, because it sends the wrong message to kids.

Back in high school, I lit up and smoked pot at lunch. I also drank heavily throughout the day. We'd cut class, and I'd hang with the jocks. One time, when I was out by the bleachers with the football crowd, I out-drank a lineman. I remember that moment. Everyone went crazy cheering me on, like I was a rock star. I was super proud of that. It was my thing.

I was a leader, even back then. If I came to a party, I'd arrive with an entourage of at least five or ten other girls. They were there because I was there. As a result, I was always one of the first people invited. No one cared that I was a little chubby.

I can't say I wasn't insecure, though. I was. I was well aware that I didn't look like the other cheerleaders. I was cute, but would never be anything like a Barbie doll. I got around it though by giving blow jobs to the boys, sometimes sex. It was a power rush to know that they were digging me for that moment. But I'd need to get drunk to do the things I did. It was probably what got me started with alcohol.

One Friday night after a big game, Josh, a jock, was fumbling with my shirt buttons at a big party at some girl's house. For all I knew, the guy was a virgin. He certainly acted like it.

"Josh," I said with my best sultry voice. "Let's go into the closet and do this thing."

His jaw dropped and all he could do was nod. I could see the bulge in his pants, and I loved that it was because of me.

I dragged my fingers slowly down his chest and unbuttoned his pants. Shit, I wasn't even wet, but I loved the Bambi look that came into his eyes. What a rush of power. I did my thing on his cock, and his eyes rolled back in his head. That boy wouldn't forget Stacy Butler any time soon.

Pimping started back then in high school. It was low-key and not really about sex. It was all about power. I'd say things like, "Go give that guy a hug so we can get some free weed."

One time, I told a hot friend, Lucy, to wear her gold bikini, put her hair down just so and then walk in front of us. She'd lure in the boys.

Since I wasn't any kind of bombshell, by no means beach material, I needed Lucy to snare them in. It wasn't like I was actually making anyone have sex at that point, but I had something these boys wanted, so if they wanted more, they had to go through me.

After high school, I went to Reading Area Community College. I had the idea that I'd get an education and do something with my life. The city of Reading was known for outlet stores, so it wasn't hard to get a job at one. I picked a shoe store. That's where I was introduced to cocaine. The girls were supposed to take the money from the store each week and deposit it. But they bought coke instead. They never got caught. No idea how they managed that. I guess no one could ever prove anything.

The minute I tried cocaine, I was hooked. I loved the stuff. It just kept me going.

It wasn't long before I left the retail field and school, but not the coke. Not the quick fix.

I liked bartending and knew I could make much better money that way. So I started working at the Silo, a local nightclub. I was about twenty by then. Lucky for me, the owner was away in Greece at the time I applied, and his nephew was running the place. I found out later that the owner only ever hired blacks for the kitchen, nothing visible like the bar. And no black was ever trusted with a register.

Unlike his uncle, the nephew was pretty open-minded. In a week, I was promoted from waitress to bartender. Three months later, when the owner returned from Greece, there I was, this black girl, behind the bar. He went ballistic. That is, until he saw how many customers were coming through, how much money I was generating. He was a business man, a smart guy, so he put up with my skin color.

Before I knew it, tolerance grew to acceptance, then friendship and genuine caring. And then he and his family loved me. He gave me the deposit for my first apartment. In fact, I had Cain's baby shower at the Silo.

That was about the time I started selling small amounts of coke in powder bags. A friend of mine, who's now doing sixty to a hundred years in jail, suggested I take bags of coke to the bar and see what I could do.

Okay!

He bagged up twenty, twenty-dollar bags (four hundred dollars' worth of coke) and only asked for two hundred back. People would come visit their favorite bartender, buy some drinks, and get a twenty-dollar bag. It was ridiculously easy. The customer just included an extra twenty when he paid for his drink, and I slipped him a little bag of coke with the drink and napkin. I sold out in ten minutes my first night. I made two hundred bucks in ten minutes.

I called my friend and told him to bring more. I was a natural.

At one point, I was bartending at three different clubs, selling coke, getting tips, and earning a thousand dollars a night. I was also kind of a celebrity back then, because I was in this all-girl rock band. I'd sing at all the local clubs, passing myself off as a black Janis Joplin. Looking back, I was a drunken mess. I thought it was cool to be like the chick in the movie, "The Rose," a drunken, powerful belter of music, with all the drugs and alcohol and shit. Of course, that chick died from her addictions, but I didn't give a shit about that.

I was dating Bobby, a deeply alcoholic man. He'd show up at my bar every night, drinking a case before we'd do coke together. I was more into the booze at that point, because I was surrounded by it all the time, drinking all night as I worked. After work, I'd continue to party for hours. That's probably what turned me into an alcoholic.

The owner of the Silo also owned a hotel called Riveredge, which was attached to the bar. This place had fancy ballrooms and banquet facilities, really nice. They'd have boxing matches there and always needed ring girls, gorgeous girls in bikinis who held up the cards between rounds. One night, they were hard up. No ring girls were available. That would lose about half the spectators. It was a disaster!

So, who'd they call?

"Stacy, can you call five of your friends to be ring girls for tonight?" The promoter sounded frantic.

"Sure," I said, without thinking. "I can do that."

The guy paused, as if unsure. "They need to be hot, you know, and wear bikinis."

"Yeah, sure," I told him. "I know what you need. I understand."

"Okay, good." He sounded so relieved.

I had him now. "I want in, though. I want a cut."

"No problem." He didn't care as long as he wasn't going to lose money that night.

I had to think fast. I picked up the phone and called five friends, and told them they had to put on skimpy swimsuits and become ring girls. It was as easy as that. It worked out really well. I got a couple hundred dollars and gave the girls something. It was easy money and it was legal. And besides that, it gave me more clout. Expanded my name. I was running those bitches and everyone knew it.

I'd walk in and the girls would come running up to me, asking me all kinds of things.

"What should I do?"

"Do I look okay?"

"Should I pose with this boxer?"

"Sure," I'd reply with a wink, "for a fee."

I quickly built up a good relationship with the promoter. He loved it because the girls I brought were so sexy. I also added extra touches, like having the girls' outfits match the boxers'. If a guy was in red, white, and blue, so was my girl's bikini.

Life seemed great back then. Bloody Marys every morning and straight bourbon at night, along with beer chasers. We had amazing cars and all of the other accessories that went along with being part of the in-crowd. I even had bodyguards I'd throw a couple of bucks to. They liked being a part of our entourage, and I liked having them around. They were my drivers, my security, and they came in handy when I started coordinating private bachelor parties. Nothing illegal, not yet, just dancing for entertainment.

My girls were so popular that they asked us to travel the boxing circuit. We went to Harrisburg, Philadelphia, and all over. It just kept getting better and better. I was making good money. I even met Don King at one point. Of course, I was drunk out of my mind, so I made a mess of it.

One time, I had a limo take a bunch of us to Philly for a boxing extravaganza. It was my birthday, so I had my hair done in corn rows, the style back then. I wore stripper heels and put the girls in slammin' outfits.

I decided that I wanted to make an extra grand, so I had the girls buy these little T-shirts and then cut them off, to show their tummies. Then I went to four different barber shops and got them to pay me two-fifty each to put their logos on the skimpy shirts. I spent that thousand on getting the girls' hair done and buying coke for everyone. I was still new to the game, so I took care of my girls.

I really wanted to be an entrepreneur, a business person, but I wasn't taken seriously because I was a woman. Sometimes, I had to fight for my money. The boxing promoters were ruthless, so I had to be, too.

I had fun with it, though, putting my own flair on things. I had some classy girls I could really dress up. One girl was especially gorgeous. She loved working as a card girl, because she didn't have to take her clothes off. She got paid well for straight work. I'd give her fifty dollars for the night, and she was in heaven. She got a limo ride, free partying, and sometimes was featured on TV to boot.

I liked that girl, so I treated her with respect. One night, I dressed her in diamonds and pearls with a sexy, elegant dress, because performance and attire were always super-important to me.

I made money off all my girls, but the one I made the most money on was my Penthouse Pet. She'd been in quite a few big adult magazines. She really added to my street cred.

One time, at a boxing match, she got an impromptu offer for a beer commercial. I was pissed because they went behind my back. They grabbed her to do the spot, trying to do an end run around me. That wasn't about to happen.

I waited for my chance and then demanded something for the use of my Penthouse Pet. In the end, they gave me five hundred dollars. It worked out.

The Queen B always got her way.

CHAPTER 5

About a week after I moved in with the John, a family friend called me.

"You still want to get into Reading Detox?"

"Shit yeah!"

"I've got an idea," she said. "Come into the ER, where I work, and tell them you can't take it anymore."

"Like…what do you mean?" I asked.

"Like tell them that you've had enough, that you're going to commit suicide."

"Shit," I said. "Okay, if that's what it takes."

Thinking it over, this was probably the only way I was going to get into the hospital and get off these drugs. So I did it. I told them that I was going to kill myself because of the drugs. Honestly, suicide was never an option, not for real, but I did feel like I was at death's door. I wasn't not sure how long I would have lasted without help.

The nurses ushered me into the back, sneaking me in. They put me in a regular hospital room because I wasn't stable enough to go through detox. They had to give me two blood transfusions and wean me off the Xanax I'd been taking, too. That stuff's addictive as hell.

After about six days, I was healthy enough to go through detox. I begged them to send me as far from Reading as possible. I didn't want to risk getting caught by the cops. They had to make special arrangements, but they did it for me and I ended up at the Pyramid Rehabilitation Center in Altoona.

The place was all girls. They figured that men were a distraction. They weren't far off on that.

The police weren't going to find me at Pyramid. I was too far away. Besides, the HIPPA law was my friend. Still, my mother managed to figure out where I was.

One day, she called me. "I'm so proud of you," she said in a soft voice I hadn't heard in some time.

"Mom," I said, closing my eyes, clinging to the phone as if it were an extension of her body. "It's so good to hear your voice. Thank you for calling! How are you and Sis doing?"

"Megan got a parking ticket last Tuesday."

"Isn't that like her third this year?"

"Yeah, something like that. Anyway, we went to the police station to pay and well, I've got some bad news."

When she didn't continue, I guessed what happened. "There's a warrant for my arrest, isn't there?" My voice choked on the last word.

She paused and then said quietly, "Yes."

It shouldn't have been a surprise. It wasn't really, but when I heard it, knew it was out there, everything became a little too real. Fear took a hold of my heart, making it hammer hard.

"Did you say anything?" I asked.

"No, of course not," she said.

"Thank you."

"They probably think you ran. I mean, that's what most people do, right?"

"Yeah, but it's not like I'll get any points for going into Rehab," I said. "The cops won't care. They just want my ass. I burned them bad."

"I just mean, I think you're safe for now."

"Probably."

"Just get through your program," she said. "Focus on that."

I was there at Pyramid for thirty days. It was boring as hell. I started wondering what I'd do when I got out. I'd have to find something completely different. I knew that, but still felt sad that I'd lost everything I'd worked so hard to build up. It hadn't *all* been bad shit, it hadn't *all* been illegal. And I'd created it all on my own…

೧೧೧

Before the shit hit the fan and I went into Pyramid, I had several ways to make money. The card-girl thing had been going well, but that wasn't enough. I became known as the one with the hot girls. People started begging me to bring my girls to their parties. Then they started asking if the girls would take off their tops.

I'd say, "Sure, if I tell them to."

It was true. They listened to me.

A whole bunch of people had complained to me about the weirdo strippers in Reading. Some of those ladies were pretty old, has-been strippers. My girls were young, fresh, and firm. And they were down with whatever I threw at them, whatever I told them to do.

I quickly made a whole new business out of the parties. I'd get at least half the money, making sure the girls got the money they needed. I'd sometimes provide the liquor and even a bartender, charging them an extra couple hundred dollars for that service.

If a client wanted a catered party, I'd make little tuna salad or egg salad finger sandwiches. I know it sounds crazy, but I went out of my way to make it nice, like I was some damned hostess. I'd charge extra for the food, of course.

I'd get some non-stripper friends to come and serve the drinks. I'd take them shopping, buy them a low-cut dress and say, "Let's go to a party."

"Sure," they'd say.

"You might have to serve a drink or two," I'd say, "but they'll tip you. You'll make some cash." I never had to pay those girls.

I did some real VIP parties for a famous rapper at the Silo. I did a whole bunch of things, but as time rolled on, my upscale ring-card-girls business changed focus. It became all about strippers, because there was more money there.

Fuck, I was the one who turned those girls into strippers.

That's about the time I started working at the Second Story Lounge strip club, as a sort of house mother. The girls would give me some of their tip money and I'd help them keep organized. I learned the business fast.

I still had my Penthouse Pet. She was a featured dancer at the Second Story. She'd have eight-by-ten glossies that she'd sign, charging fifty bucks a pop. Since I'd be the one selling the pictures, I developed a pitch.

"Yeah, these pictures are fifty bucks," I'd say, "but how would you like to talk with her?"

Their eyes would pop. "Yeah, that would be great!"

"I could arrange that. She'll come over and sit with you for another twenty-five." They loved that and so I'd pocket a cool twenty-five dollars a person.

She wouldn't just do any private party, only big-timers. I had some big-time clientele, who would pay thousands for a private party with her. Then I'd rake in the money.

I started working at a second strip club, a place called the Adam's Apple, which was owned by another Greek man. He was very old school Greek. He knew Frank Sinatra and was into Thoroughbred horses, the whole nine yards. He didn't approve of my doing cocaine, but looked the other way. He liked me.

That man taught me a lot about business, letting me run the upstairs fine dining restaurant. He would leave at nine and that's when the place would turn into coke central. Before I arrived on the scene, another man dealt coke out of the Adam's Apple. He thought it was his turf, but I quickly taught him otherwise.

The thing is that having women pretty much trumps everything. Since I had women and coke and he just had coke, I won out easily. On top of that, he couldn't help himself, he'd come to me for women. He was just another trick, so no one saw him as anything much. He needed me, but I didn't need him.

My boss asked me if I wanted to do anything with the downstairs. There was nothing going on downstairs, so I started my own club. Trying to be nice, I asked the other coke guy if he wanted to work with me and he flatly refused. He didn't want to have any part of it if I was involved. That was for the best. I told my boss I was in.

So I finally had my own place, which was a total rush. I could call all the shots. The first thing I did was install two poles. You've got to have poles if you're running a strip club. Then I started to get creative, doing something I always wanted to do. Inspired by the 1982 movie *Night Shift*, I installed a really cool swing. The Queen B wanted a swing, so they installed one.

The place was small and quaint. We had round tables with white linen. In the center of each table were two candles, one red, one white. The clientele were all bigtime drug dealers from Reading and New York. I had a door man, who'd only allow in people I Okayed. This all took place after the fine dining restaurant closed, of course. Fine dining and strippers didn't mix.

The show started out being very classy and elegant. I'd have the girls come out in beautiful robes and gowns. They'd do their thing, making all the men drool. Guys would throw dollars on the stage, begging to see the girls. I'd wait until there was at least fifty bucks on the floor and that's when I'd tell them to take their clothes off.

In those days, I was more like a madam.

A lot of people don't realize that there's a difference between a madam and a pimp. A madam encourages the women and dotes on the men. A pimp doesn't give a shit about anyone. Pimps are brutal. I started out as a madam and wound up a pimp.

My place closed at midnight. Staying open any later caused too much trouble. Since the bars stayed open until two in the morning, they would bribe me to come to them after hours. When I came, my girls and clients would follow. It was good business. I had my entourage, so these

clubs would pay me to sit in their establishments and drink.
As soon as I walked into any club, the DJ would play Jennifer Lopez's song, "I'm Real." It was a respect thing. DJs have a thing about playing songs twice in a row, but I'd throw down a C-note and yell, "Play it again!"
And they would. Women hated it and men ate it up.
Sometimes, I'd sing along with the lyrics. "My life, I live it, to the limit, an' I love it!"
We'd walk in with fur coats and take over the place. No one could say anything. There was always a lot of cocaine going on. I'd get all sorts of free coke and the girls would do anything I told them to, because they were so strung out. I made them that way.
I kept the prostitution side of things super hush-hush in the beginning. It really started at the Adam's Apple, where I told myself that whatever happened in the backroom had nothing to do with me. I'd just get broken off from the top.
A guy might say, "I want to go in the back room with Jacquie."
"Sure," I'd say, "give me a hundred bucks and I'll make it happen."
Then he'd get to go back with the girl for twenty minutes. I didn't care what they paid her, I didn't care what they were doing. I stayed out of it. I told myself that whatever they did was up to them.

There were girls I'd only let go in the back room, girls that weren't good enough for the front. They just weren't hot enough for the stage. But they were just fine for the back.

I remember this one girl, Maya, that worked hard for me. In the business, she'd be called my "bottom bitch." She was the girl that would do anything, and I mean anything. I knew that and so I'd manipulate her like crazy. She stayed with me a long time, even up to when I worked out of my home on Birch Street.

There was this very good customer who owned a car lot. He'd launder his money through me, hundred dollar bills. I had no idea what he was doing, but I didn't give a shit. I just wanted his money. Later, I found out he got caught and did a lot of time.

So one day, he stopped by my home on Birch Street and asked, "Do you think you could get Maya to come out here and give me a blow job?"

"Sure," I said. That was the first time I'd ever had anyone ask me in those terms, so upfront and direct. However, this guy was at my front door, asking for a blow job. It took me a whole two seconds before I could reply. "A hundred dollars for ten minutes," I told him.

"Done," he said.

"Okay, give me the hundred and I'll make it happen."

He went back to his car and waited. I went and found Maya. "You're going to go outside and give this guy a blow job. When you're done, I'll give you fifty dollars. Understand?"

"Okay," she said.

She didn't question it. Ten minutes later she came back in and got her money. Shit, I made fifty bucks in ten minutes and didn't do a thing for it.

That's pretty much the point where things went downhill and fast. Once you start doing things like that, selling sex directly, you get known for it. People stop caring about the gowns, the classy linen, and the artistic swing. They just want sex.

Even the girls started saying, "Why would I dance for dollars when I can just go suck a guy's dick for a lot more?" They didn't want to waste their time.

ⰭⰮⰭ

It was hard to believe now that I was giving it all up for real.

The rehab was a bit of a blur. I had plenty of time to think about the past, think about all the shit I'd done, in those thirty days I was in Pyramid.

Well, that life was all behind me now. I had no idea what the future would bring, but one thing was for sure. The Queen B was getting her act together for the first time.

CHAPTER 6

When I successfully completed my program at Pyramid, I had to find a recovery house. Some people tried to go out on their own after the rehab, but I knew better. I'd just revert. I needed support. Not surprisingly, Mom refused to take me in. I couldn't blame her. I wouldn't have taken me in either.

The people at Pyramid found a recovery house in Reading on Perkiomen Avenue. It was a good choice, because I didn't associate that part of town with getting high. That was important. I hadn't grown up there either, which helped.

I needed to do a telephone interview to get in. Georgia, a nice-sounding woman, asked me a bunch of questions. It went well, so she offered me a place in her home. She told me about the restored mansion, which had seven apartments. It sounded beautiful.

But I wasn't going anywhere without Cain. I'd been away from him for thirty days and missed the hell out of him. CYS allowed me to take him, because they could monitor us there at the home.

I took a bus from Pyramid back to Reading. Mom and Cain picked me up at the station. The first thing I did was swoop Cain into my arms and hug him tight. He didn't want to let go, and neither did I.

All I had was what I was wearing and a single trash bag of clothing to my name. That's it. No money, no food, no nothing. I was starting over.

A beautiful white woman in her late-forties with curly dark hair greeted me at the door of the recovery house. She introduced herself as Delores, the house mother, explaining that she lived there. I felt at ease immediately with her.

She took me downstairs to pick out my shower curtain and linens, before showing me my new gorgeous, spotless apartment. It had everything I needed, two beds, two dressers, and clean appliances. Coming from the Birch Street place, which was so dark and dirty, this home was a blessing from God. It was a second chance.

Of course, in my mind, I was still the Queen B, the master manipulator. I wasn't over that mindset, with a mere thirty days of being clean and sober under my belt. This was just my next move. I was still bad-assed.

The Queen B deserved a lovely home like this. I'd been through rehab and wasn't going to any bullshit

YMCA. No, Stacy Butler was getting the Rolls Royce of recovery houses. That was how it should be.

Even though Delores was sweet and kind, she wasn't weak. Behind those striking blue eyes was a woman who'd done hard time in jail. She knew all the cons and wasn't taking any bullshit. That's exactly what the Queen B needed. I knew I couldn't get away with anything and didn't even really try. She'd done jail time and I respected that.

Georgia, the woman I'd talked to on the phone, came over the next day to introduce herself. She looked different than I'd imagined her. Her stark white face was framed with short dark hair. I guessed she was in her sixties, but her tailored suit and makeup made her look younger. She let me know right from the start that she'd done jail time as well. "I heard about you. I did my research. They used to call you the Queen B on the street," she said, looking down at me through her wire-framed glasses.

"That's right," I said, trying to sound humble.

"Yeah, well, guess what? There's only one Queen Bitch around here and that's me."

She immediately put me on restrictions. She told me not to make any plans for the weekend. I would be confined to the house.

The recovery house was extremely firm, but I didn't fight against it at all. I had nowhere else to go, no choices, so the last thing I wanted was to get kicked out of this place. And I wanted my kid with me.

Still, it pissed me off. Who was Georgia to talk to the Queen B like that? That fucking bitch!

Fuming, I called Mom. "I don't think this is going to work out," I muttered into the receiver. I had a fantasy that if I complained enough, maybe she'd rescue me, pay for an apartment or let me come home to her place. Anything was better than this place with Georgia, the tyrant.

"Well, it had better work out!" Mom shouted into the phone. "You don't have another choice, prima donna. You're not the Queen B anymore."

"They took my cell." I knew I was whining, but I couldn't help it.

"Good!"

"But Mom," I said, "they're telling me I can't wear makeup or go out this weekend."

"What did you expect?"

"But Mom—"

"Stay there!" She hung up.

I was pissed at her, pissed at Georgia, and pissed at the world. Who the hell was she to turn me away? It didn't take long for me to cool down and realize that Mom was right. Besides, she was done with me and all the shit I put her through. It was a good thing she didn't cave and bail me out.

I found out that there were three warrants for my arrest. I was a wanted woman. As luck would have it,

Rhonda, one of the other girls living at the recovery house, had a mom who was an attorney. It turned out that her mom, Kate, was also a family friend.

Rhonda and I called her together.

"I have Stacy on the phone. What should we do?"

"Stacy, you're going to have to turn yourself in, immediately." Her voice was clipped, but she sounded kind.

"I figured," I said, resigned to my fate.

"Look," she said. "I'll be there in the morning to pick you up. It won't be easy, but I'll be there every step of the way with you."

I got lucky, because they could have arrested me right then and there. But Kate pled my case, saying I'd be in a closed environment, that I wasn't going anywhere. In the end, I had to go to three district justice offices in order to be let go on my own recognizance.

I went back to the house and waited. I had to go to a few preliminary hearings, but we kept waiving them, so the DA started waiving them, too. I started thinking about my old boss from the Adam's Apple. I was glad he couldn't see me now. He would have never approved of any of my shit...

෴

When he passed away back in 2004, things had gotten much worse for me at the time. I never owned anything, not even the liquor license. I worked through his.

He made everything legit and I ran his business. So when he passed, the liquor license disappeared, as did the club. I was left with nothing.

Everything changed instantly. I went from dining on crab and doing ounces and ounces of cocaine to scrounging for value meals and having to find money for drugs. That's when I met very seedy people, who would come to my house and pay for sex from my girls, the girls who used to work at the Adam's Apple.

Gone were the linens and pretty candles. In their place was the glow of crack pipes. We had no liquor license, but plenty of booze kept flowing. It wasn't long before I had turned the Birch Street house into a brothel.

That was when I discovered crack. Jill, a girl I knew through the club, would come over and smoke crack at my house. I figured what the hell and gave it a try.

The high was way better. I couldn't believe the euphoria. It was wild! I wanted to get out and do things, at a million miles an hour. I knew crack was the bottom of the barrel, but I didn't care. It was an amazing high, way worth it.

With Jill, came her friend, Black, a big black man who would do crack with us. He'd give it to me at first then seduce me with it. He loved to put me in a sleeper hold, knocking me out. He got off on that. He'd knock me out and I'd wake up a little later to see him sitting at the dining room table eating dinner. He'd laugh out loud at how disoriented I'd look.

He loved to beat me. One day, he snapped my right arm like it was a twig. He'd get off on raping me, hurting me. The sex with him was violent. I hated it, but loved the attention. I was addicted to him.

If I ever thought about giving up crack, even for a day, he'd laugh. One time, I was washing dishes and he came up from behind and grabbed my nipples hard. "You're a dirty little crack head," he whispered in my ear.

I gritted my teeth against the pain. "You know what?" I told him. "I'm not going to do that shit today. You can keep your crack."

He laughed and left the room. I started making dinner, chicken paprika, something I did well. He came back in, sat at the table, and lit up a pipe. He caught my hungry look and laughed. "Oh, so you're not doing it today. Is that right?"

I couldn't help myself. When he offered me a hit, I took it. He laughed at me, but I didn't care. I was gone. Then he raped me.

I found out later that Black had nine kids. He ended up in jail for not paying any child support, of all things. In his own way, I think he liked me. When I was in rehab, he wrote to warn me that the cops were looking for me.

He even tried to visit me at the recovery house, but Delores wouldn't let him in. I broke the rules, though, and met him the next day. I don't know why I was so stupid. I was off pot, cocaine, and alcohol, but I guess I forgot that Black was just another drug. It was a mistake that nearly cost me everything. When Delores found out, she slammed me hard, putting me on restrictions, so if I wanted to leave the house, I needed a buddy.

I shook with fear when I realized that slip nearly cost me the hard-fought trust I'd built up at the recovery house. Shit, I couldn't afford that. I turned it around, though, and never saw Black again. Staying clean and sober was too important.

CHAPTER 7

I needed money, I needed a job. Actually, it wasn't just about making money. I wanted to do something with my time, do something that might help others. I wasn't picky about what I did, but I hoped I might find work in a restaurant. I liked the idea of serving people.

I'd become close friends with a few of the girls at the recovery house. Ginny, a skinny white woman, lived on my floor and we'd bonded. She worked at the Charcoal Chef as a waitress. When I told her I was looking for work, she agreed to keep an eye open for me.

One day, she came back to the house, exhausted. She plopped down on the chair across from me. "No one showed up for work today."

"Really?" I tried to not let my excitement show, but this was good news.

She rubbed her right foot. "I can't handle all those tables myself, no matter what Anen says."

Anen was the Egyptian owner and cook. I'd been in there a few times, but had never talked to him. He was always super busy in the kitchen.

"Maybe he could use some help," I said.

"Yeah, that's what I was thinking. Why don't you come in tomorrow and we'll see if we can't get you hired?" Ginny said. "It's a good place to work. The food's good and I love it there."

"I know you do," I said. "That's good enough for me!"

Ginny got free meals there sometimes and brought me home leftovers. It was good Pennsylvania Dutch home style cooking, just like my Pappy used to make.

She shrugged. "Anen's gruff, but fair. And they haven't changed the menu since 1952. There's stability there. It's nice."

"Sounds good," I responded.

The next morning, I followed Ginny to the Charcoal Chef. The place was on the same street as the recovery house. It was an oddly shaped building with a huge yellow and red sign popping up from the top like a chimney. It still had that old 1950's look.

My pulse raced. I wanted this, but knew it wouldn't be easy. People don't want to hire you when you live at a recovery house, especially if you're on your way to jail. Most people wouldn't take a chance on someone like me.

The turnover was high, but it was like that anywhere. When I walked in, I felt like I'd entered a time warp. Most of the patrons were elderly.

"I'm going to like it here," I whispered to Ginny.

She squeezed my arm and walked up to the olive-skinned man behind the counter. "Anen, this is my friend, Stacy. She's looking for work," she said.

The man glared at me. "I don't think so." He didn't want any part of my black self.

I turned to leave, but Ginny pulled me back.

"Anen," she said, adopting a soft sweet voice. "Come on now, you know I need the help. Geraldine and Monica quit. I can't run all these tables myself."

Anen's lips tightened, but he didn't say no. His eyes fixated on me. Encouraged by his silence, Ginny said, "Let her try out for one day. If you're not happy, I won't ask again."

I stayed quiet, trying to steady my breathing. I waited what seemed like forever for the man to give an uncertain nod. He turned back to cooking and that was that. I had my chance.

I picked up the menu and looked it over. There were five pages of items, densely packed in. It was a lot to learn.

"You'll get the hang of it," Ginny whispered. "Besides, the customers know it by heart. At least, most of them do."

"Thanks, Ginny."

"No sweat," she said. She nodded at a couple that looked to be in their seventies. "Why don't you start with Harold and Becky? They're sweethearts."

I walked over to them and took a deep breath. "Hello, I'm Stacy. I'm new here. What would you like?"

Becky was a slight white woman with kind brown eyes. "Welcome, Stacy! Harold and I always get the same thing."

She rattled off the order and I wrote it down. I repeated it back to her, just to make sure I got it right. She winked her approval.

When I brought them their breakfast, Harold confided in me that he and his wife started coming to the Charcoal Chef when they were courting, some fifty years ago. "We're sentimental creatures," he said.

Many of the customers were as lovely as this couple. I realized that if I played my cards right, I could possibly find a home at the Charcoal Chef. I worked hard to learn the ropes.

Ginny gave me four tables to start, allowing me to get my footing. Anen didn't praise me, but he also didn't yell at me. I figured silence was a good thing.

The lunch rush kept us busy, but I made sure to add some extra touches. When I saw someone with a walker, I'd rush over and offer assistance. When some of the men were hunched over, I offered to rub their backs. They loved that.

I started feeling more and more comfortable and realized it would be a good idea to introduce myself to the regulars. I took to explaining that I was just like them, with a strong Pennsylvania Dutch upbringing. Sometimes, I mentioned my Pappy and talked about how he'd made pepper cabbage almost as good as Anen did.

By the time we closed the restaurant, I was everyone's new favorite waitress. Anen grunted that I could come back the next day. It was a real job! Anen and I never became friends, but he kept me on. He was a business man and I was good for business.

The Charcoal Chef was a good, wholesome, drug-free environment—something I desperately needed. I still got social security for Cain and me, so I was doing okay financially.

Mom came by the recovery house on a regular basis. She'd bring stuff for all the girls and, of course, Cain. Most of them didn't have much of anything, and no family to look after them. Mom took over as a surrogate mother. Both Delores and Georgia became close to her as well.

I started attending recovery meetings three to five times a week. It was a point of sanity for me. I met a beautiful-looking man there, Ken. He was bald with big muscles and lived at ADAPPT, a halfway house. We'd meet half way and go to the meetings together.

Ken had been in jail for twenty-two years. After twenty years, he got out on parole, but went right back in for a parole violation. He treated me like a princess.

One day, we met at a coffee house on the way to a meeting. He pulled out a small burgundy box and handed it to me.

"What's this?" I asked.

He blushed. "A present."

I opened the box and saw a beautiful gold watch inside. It must have cost a small fortune. My eyes flew up to pierce his blue ones.

"When did you buy this?" I asked. "You just got out of jail."

"Two years ago. I had it in storage. I bought it together with this one," he said, extending his arm to reveal the matching watch.

"Why did you buy a women's watch?" I asked. He didn't have a girlfriend two years ago. It seemed like an odd purchase.

"I always knew I'd find you," he murmured into my ear.

He stole my heart with that statement. I kissed him hard, pushing myself up against him. He felt so good.

Over the next couple months, we'd talk on the phone for hours. He hadn't wasted his time in jail, but had studied law. He could file motions and offer advice to fellow inmates. Jail either preserves you or breaks you down, I always say.

"Stacy, all I ever wanted was to have a family," he'd say to me. "I want a little girl and a wife to love. I want to take care of you."

He'd teach me things. Part of the reason I have the vocabulary I do today is because of Ken. I learned to love words and appreciate the English language.

The recovery house had become my home, but the rule was that you could only stay there nine months. It wasn't supposed to be a permanent thing, just a bridge-gap for real life. Unfortunately, that time was coming to an end.

Mom had helped save some of my social security money for me, so I actually had a few thousand dollars with which to move out and pay first and last months' rent and a security deposit.

I found a little apartment on Eckert Ave, right near the recovery house and the Charcoal Chef. I wanted to be close to where I had been doing well, so that if things got bad, I could go back and get help.

Ken wanted to move in with me. He was up for release from ADAPPT and needed a home plan, a place to live that made sense to his parole officer. We'd only been together for a month, but I was already madly in love with him. So I agreed.

His parole officer came over to do the home plan check. He sat me down, a hard look in his eyes. This wasn't going to be a pleasant conversation.

"Do you know Ken's a convicted murderer?" he asked without preamble.

I bristled. *Of course!* I reminded myself that this man was trying to help me. "Yes, I know."

"The first sentence was ten years for third degree murder," he said. "Then he stayed another ten for attempted murder inside the prison. Were you aware of that?"

I nodded. Ken had been honest with me. "Yes."

"But I bet you don't know who he tried to knock off."

I shook my head. "I didn't ask."

"It was a hate crime," the man said. "Ken was a Nazi skin head. He tried to kill a black guy."

I hadn't known that. Still, I loved my man. "Look, Ken loves me. It's fine. He's changed. We go to recovery meetings together. I know what I'm doing."

"Just be careful. You're a black woman with a black son."

He wasn't the only one to warn me. Lots of people thought living with an ex-con like Ken was a bad idea. The woman that ran the halfway house where he lived sat me down and had a similar conversation.

In the end, I ignored everyone's advice and let Ken move into the little apartment on Eckert St. He carried my bed on his back down the street because I didn't have a car. Sweat was dripping down his back in the hot August sun. What a gorgeous specimen of a man!

Deep down, I knew that it was too early for me to hook up with a guy. I'd been sober less than a year and wasn't the greatest judge of character. Just look at my past picks. Still, I was in love.

Sure enough, by Christmas he was back to getting drunk all the time. Since he stayed away from drugs, I didn't kick him out. I couldn't stand the thought of losing him. I was hooked, addicted to him.

I did tell him that he couldn't bring the alcohol home. He'd respect that, but he wasn't a nice drunk. He'd get mad and hit cars, yelling all kinds of things out on the street.

Sex was weird with him. I guess because he was in jail so long he probably masturbated all the time, or maybe he had anal sex with other inmates. We never talked about it. He just couldn't keep an erection with me for long. We'd rarely finish sex, with him pre-ejaculating, unless he finished himself off first.

Despite that, I found myself pregnant in December. She was truly a miracle, because I'd had a gastric bypass and was told there was no way I'd get pregnant again. I'd always wanted a girl, so I was happy. When Ken found out, he was so excited that he actually stayed sober for a while.

"I was like an animal in jail," he'd say, touching my belly. "Now you're going to make my dreams come true. We're going to be a family."

I cried, thinking that this miracle baby was going to save her father's life. He might actually turn a corner and stay away from the booze this time.

Around that time, Anen sold the Charcoal Chef to a Greek woman named Effie. The minute she walked in, I knew we'd be friends. She had owned Effie's Pizza Villa, but when her husband was murdered, she needed a change of environment. I was thrilled when she agreed to keep me on.

"Effie," I asked her, "if you're still running this place when I get out of prison, can I work for you again?"

"If you do the right thing," Effie said, "you can have your job back."

It was right then, when I was happy, feeling like everything was working out for me, that I got a call saying that Ken had been pulled over for a DUI. My whole world suddenly crashed down. In order to bail him out of jail, I found myself in the middle of the city at midnight, something I hadn't done since my Queen B days. I was scared, being at risk big time. A person out on their own recognizance, awaiting trial, shouldn't be doing this.

After I bailed him out, he shouted, "Those motherfuckers!"

"Ken," I said, "Shhh."

"They're trying to frame me," he said, looking around the room frantically.

"Let's just go home," I said.

"I'm a killer. Don't they know?" he shouted.

I took him home. He'd be going back to jail now for sure. He had to turn himself in to his parole officer on Valentine's Day.

"Stacy, I'm gonna run," he told me.

I shook my head. "If you go on the run, you'll lose me and your baby forever."

"Stacy—"

"Look, if you go and turn yourself in, they may put you in rehab. You never know. If all goes well, maybe, just maybe you can take our baby when I have to go to jail. She needs her daddy," I pleaded with him.

Most guys would have run, but he decided to do the right thing. He didn't want to lose me and lose the only chance he'd ever have for a family. He turned himself in. I expected him to and he did. The messed up thing was, they sent him back upstate. No second chances. That's the way it goes. That poor guy had grown up in jail and was headed back.

My jury trial was scheduled in two weeks. I hoped things would go better for me. I lay awake at night, thinking about how I was facing five to ten years, pregnant with my miracle girl.

Please God, let the jury go easy on me!

CHAPTER 8

When I stepped into the courtroom, I felt a surge of hope. Maybe I could get out of all this and go back home to my family. I was praying that they'd give me a ton of community hours to serve. I'd love that, helping others and being free.

The Pennsylvania Prison Society showed up to be there for me. They're a non-profit group, founded back when the Declaration of Independence was signed, promoting a humane approach to justice. My story was compelling, being that I was clean and sober and heavy with child.

It started out really well. The twelve men and women in the jury box were eating up my story. It was good. Here I was, a bad girl turned good, with a strong proven track record of reform. Who can resist a comeback kid?

Tonya, the trooper, even came out and testified. She explained to the jury, how when one of our transactions was five dollars short, I had paid her back.

"It shows her character," she said. "Stacy wasn't all bad."

A few of them nodded and my heart leapt in my chest. I always said I was an honest hustler, if there really is such a thing.

There was a fleeting moment when I thought that maybe, just maybe, they'd give me a chance and it would all work out. Looking into the jurors' eyes, I could see they didn't want to send me to prison.

But then the DA had his turn and everything turned upside down.

He went on and on about all the things I had done. It was horrible, hearing everything he said. It was all true and I felt like sinking through the floor.

When the DA was done, the judge gave the jury very strict instructions. They had to go back into the jury room and decide what to do based *solely* on the law, not their feelings. That took away any shot I had for any sort of second chance. The law was the law. There was no way around it, I was going to jail.

I had quite an entourage in the hallway of the Berks County Courthouse. There were thirty or so people there for me, all waiting for the verdict. My Aunt Martha prayed along with my support group and all my friends. I still get goose bumps when I think of how much all those people loved and supported me.

When the bailiff came out and informed us that the jury was back, I almost lost the contents of my stomach. I walked into the courtroom and not a single juror looked me in the eye. I knew that wasn't a good sign.

Please look at me!

If I screamed loud enough in my mind, maybe I could somehow get a few of them to turn their heads through sheer willpower. It didn't work. They steadily avoided looking anywhere close to my vicinity, as I stood at the table waiting for the judge to speak.

"Ladies and gentlemen of the jury, have you reached a unanimous verdict?" the judge asked.

Look at me!

The foreman looked up at him. "Yes, your honor."

Please!

"How do you find as to count one of the indictment, charging the defendant with conspiracy to possess cocaine with intent to distribute?"

"Guilty."

The foreman's voice was clear and direct. Although he wasn't loud, the sound of that single word reverberated through the stone room and rung in my skull. Of course, I had tried to prepare myself for that verdict, but I couldn't predict the effect it would have on me. The shock made breathing difficult.

What's going to happen to me? What's going to happen to my baby?

As they read each count, the foreman pronounced me guilty each time. There were nine counts. Each time he read the word *guilty,* it felt like someone was punching me in the face. I could almost see flashes, like when Jessie beat me up.

It was over quickly, too quickly. My head was spinning when the DA dropped the next bombshell. "Your honor, we'd like to request immediate sentencing."

What? No! I need time!

God answered my prayer.

"We request a continuance of sentencing, your honor," my lawyer said. His voice was calm and confident. "She has a job and a son. She needs time to put her life in order."

The Prison Society jumped in, trying to get the judge to extend the continuance to allow me to have my baby outside of prison, but he wouldn't go for it. The DA wanted my head, but I was given until April 20th to turn myself in for sentencing. The DA's parting words that day were, "Your honor, we request to make Ms. Butler's sentences consecutive, not concurrent."

I felt my knees buckle and the room started moving on its own.

If the judge followed that request, it could mean twenty years in jail. They had originally told me five to ten before trial. Consecutive would mean I would never be able to be a mom to my baby girl.

The fear of my final sentencing hung over my head like some crazy cartoon anvil, but at least I had a reprieve, time to sort things out. I went home to chill. When Ken called me from prison, I was a wreck. I told him what happened.

"Stacy, I'm sorry," he said.

"Yeah," was all I could muster.

"Look, sweetheart, if you use, I'll understand," he said.

I pulled the receiver away from my ear and stared at it in disbelief. The father of my baby was suggesting I take drugs. Reluctantly, I put it back to my ear. "How could you say that? I'm carrying your baby!"

"I know, but I just—"

"I'm not going to use. And I'm not running." I hung up the phone. Talking to Ken wasn't a good idea.

My recovery people all called me and begged me not to use. They expected me to, so they called around the clock. Frustrated and depressed, I stopped answering the phone after a while and just lay there in the dark. Tears didn't form, because I couldn't really process what was happening.

Guilty! Guilty! Guilty! The incessant chant plagued me as I lay there.

When I wouldn't pick up the phone, people started coming over. They all expected me to relapse. It's what addicts do.

My little miracle baby saved my life. There was no way I was going to harm her, so using was out of the question. That little life growing inside me stopped me from even considering it. People finally figured that out and left me alone.

My thoughts turned to Cain, who was almost eleven. I did my best to prepare him, but there was really no way to explain it to him. And I was a mess most of the time, waiting for sentencing.

One day, he came into the living room when I'd been crying all day. "What's wrong, Mom?" he asked. When I didn't answer immediately, he asked, "Jail again?"

"Yeah," I managed to get out between the sobs. "Cain, I need to make sure you understand what's about to happen. Do you know that Mommy's going away on April 20th for a long time?"

"Yeah, I know," he said. "You're going to jail."

"That's right," I said.

"Oh well, you shouldn't have did drugs in 2003 and 2004." He was just so exact about the whole thing. "You're getting your consequences."

He was right.

I made arrangements for Cain to stay with my sister and mother. However, neither of them were equipped to take a newborn. After giving it all a lot of thought, I asked Georgia to take care of my daughter while I was in prison. She agreed. It wasn't like I had a ton of choices. The fact was, she was my only option.

"Just promise me that you won't let her call you 'Mommy,' okay?" I asked her.

"Sure, I promise," she said.

"And tell her about me. I want her to know that her mommy loves her."

"I'll take real good care of her, like she was my own daughter."

"Thank you," I replied.

"Still," she said, "you know with welfare and all, it would be much easier for me if you could sign over your rights to her while you're in prison."

A chill of fear shot down my spine at the thought of signing over my rights to my baby girl. I trusted Georgia, but not that much. I wanted my daughter when I got out. I had to be careful, though, because I needed Georgia. The last thing I wanted to do was offend her.

"Georgia, I can't do that," I said, keeping my voice as light and cheerful as I could. "She's my daughter and always will be my daughter. It's really important that baby Melissa always knows that."

"Oh, I know," Georgia said with a nervous laugh. "I just meant paperwork-wise, it would be easier, that's all. It would be no big deal, though."

"But it is a big deal to me," I said, taking a deep but ragged breath.

How can I explain this so she'll understand?

Finally, I hit upon it. "I never want her to think for a second that I gave her up, even if it is just on paper."

"Ah, okay, I understand," she said. "No problem. We'll work around any difficulties that might come up."

I could sense that she was accepting what I was saying. It was important that she continue to be happy with the arrangement.

"It's such a relief to know that you'll be taking care of my baby," I said to her. "It means everything to me to know that she'll have a safe place to live while I finish my sentence."

I meant every word. Without Georgia, the state would have adopted her out to someone else, because they'd consider her abandoned. She'd have been put in the system and I would have never seen her again.

Over the next two weeks, a couple of federal agents came around a couple times, asking me if I had any information on some multiple murder cases they had. I told them what I knew. I wanted to help out. After all, I used to hang with murderers and rapists and they knew it.

I continued to go to work until the day I went to jail. A few weeks before sentencing, I gave away a ton of my stuff. There was no way to store it all. I invited my friend Madison over, so I could unload my best items to her.

"You sure, sweetie?" she asked when I handed her boxes of books and things.

I shrugged. "What am I going to do with all this stuff, anyway?"

She shook her head. "You're so upbeat about everything."

"What choice do I have? I'm free now, right? I should make the most of it, I figure."

"Hey, let's forget all of this for a while and take Cain to Ikea," she suggested.

My eyes lit up. "Yeah, sounds good."

Ikea was always my favorite store. I could wander for hours and just look at all the set-ups. Cain loved their cafeteria. The Swedish meatballs were his favorite. He'd always count them all before popping them in his mouth. Then, he'd ask for a second plate.

"Did you know how jealous I was of you when we were kids?" I asked Madison.

"No," she said. "Were you?"

"Yeah. Remember when my mom was pregnant with Megan and *your* mom was having *twins*?" I said with a grin.

"Sure."

"Well, I didn't like that your mom trumped mine!"

Madison burst out laughing. "I guess two beats one, right?"

"You got that right," I said. I looked around and sighed. I kind of knew I was creating a memory that would need to last me awhile. I needed to take the time to appreciate the freedom I'd always taken for granted.

As the sentencing date approached, I did my best to keep my thoughts positive, but I knew I wouldn't be coming home. I kissed Cain the morning of April 20th and cried. I had no idea when I'd kiss him again.

The sentencing hearing was a whirl. All I could really hear was the sound of my heartbeat whooshing in my ears. Afterward, two female officers cuffed me and escorted me down a hallway. My attorney followed.

"Stacy," he said gently. "Do you know what just happened?"

"No," I said. I could feel my knees buckling. "I have no idea."

"You got four to eight years," he said.

The DA didn't get his way. That was a huge relief. Okay, four years was something I could live with. The lawyer left, and before long, I found myself in front of a holding cell in the basement of the courthouse.

"Welcome to the dungeon," one of the officers said as he un-cuffed me. "Watch your step."

I rubbed my wrists and stepped inside the concrete cage. I had on a dress and heels, which was a little awkward with my big belly. I laid down on the hard concrete step inside. It wasn't comfortable, but I was exhausted. The guard brought me a peanut butter sandwich and a few peanut butter cookies. I guess since I was pregnant, they wanted to feed me a little protein.

Later that day, they shackled me again to bring me to the showers. They inspected every orifice, which was very embarrassing, especially since I was pregnant. Looking around, I supposed this was a normal Friday night for some of these people.

Not for me, I silently sulked.

When they were done probing me, they let me dress and walked me to a bus, which would take me to Berks County Prison. As I walked along the corridor, I suddenly felt dizzy.

"Can we stop for a second?" I asked.

"Sure thing, sugar," the lady officer said. She found a chair and let me catch my breath.

"Thank you," I said.

"How many years did you get?"

"Four," I whispered. I looked up at her. "I'm two years sober and five months pregnant."

She gave a low whistle. "I can't believe that. What's going to happen to your baby when you deliver?"

"Someone's going to come and get her," I reassured her.

"Oh, that's good," she said. "That way she'll be waiting for you when you get out."

I nodded and stood up. "Okay, I'm ready to go now."

The ride to Berks was unremarkable. When we got there, I was quarantined for five days. They can't let anyone into the population without knowing if she has some kind of transmittable disease. Normally, they'd put me with other people during the quarantine, but they didn't want to risk it, being that I was pregnant. So they put me in the hole, a place people who have behavioral issues go. People try to hurt themselves in the hole. It's the worst place in jail.

When I got to the hole, there was someone else there. Since there was only one bed, they brought me a yoga mat to sleep on.

My first night in jail and I'm on an exercise mat, on the floor, in the hole.

People were banging on the walls, some were screaming at the top of their lungs. One might think that the hole is a dark place, like a medieval dungeon or something. It isn't. Horrid fluorescent lights were on steadily, day and night. I only had one tiny square window on my door.

When I woke up the next day, I looked at the girl in my cell. She was a slender black girl in her late twenties.

Shit, four more days to go.

"What you in here for?" I asked.

She burst into tears. "Traffic tickets."

"What?" I tried to keep a straight face. *Traffic tickets?* "How long are you here for?"

"Four days," she said. "They can't let me into the main area, 'cause I've got to be quarantined like everyone else. I hate this place."

"Me, too," I said. "I'm Stacy. What's your name?"

"Judy," she said. "I miss my son." She dissolved into a fresh pool of tears.

"I have a kid, too," I told her.

"Yeah, how old?" she asked.

"He's eleven," I said. "Cain's his name. I'm in here for four years and I'm pregnant, so don't feel so bad." I gave her a pat on the arm and a small smile. "You could be me!"

She laughed. "Yeah, that would suck. I guess I should be grateful."

"How'd you get jail time for a traffic violation anyway?" I asked.

"I'm always speeding," she said with a shrug. "Last time, I had to go before a judge. He stuck me in here to teach me some kind of lesson."

"Fuck him," I said.

She smiled and said, "We can share the bed if you want. I'll take the floor tonight. I mean you're pregnant and all."

So, the hole wasn't so bad after all.

Soon, I went to overflow, which was a huge dorm-room-like place, with something like fifty beds in it. Judy got to go home and I thought about how she'd get to see her son.

When would I see Cain?

Overflow had about twenty women. I think they were the good inmates. Since it was my first offense, I wasn't considered a behavioral problem, so they let me into overflow.

By some good fortune, my friend Missy just happened to be in there. We'd known each other for years. I couldn't believe my eyes when I saw her large white frame.

"Stacy!" she shouted when she saw me. "It's the Queen B! Get your ass over here."

"You've got to tell me what to do in here," I whispered.

"No sweat," she promised with a wink. "I've been here more than once."

I quickly learned that Missy pretty much ran the jail. She was waiting out her trial and sentencing in County. I became her adopted child. People listened to her. She had clout. No one would dare hurt me under her watchful eye. It wasn't like anyone was trying to harm me, but she protected me, nonetheless.

The first shock was the food. It was really bad, I mean horrible.

"Don't eat that shit," Missy said. "You'll need money so you can buy food from the commissary. That stuff's decent."

"But I don't have any money," I said.

"Don't worry, I'll feed you." And she did. She didn't have much, but what she did have, she shared. My favorite turned out to be something called chichi soup. You took Top Ramon noodles and put cheese curls and wet potato chips on it. Then you nuked it in the microwave and it actually tasted good, like baked potato and noodles, with cheese.

It's funny to think back about the caviar and lobster I used to dine on back in the days of the Queen B. Still, I don't know if that ever tasted as good as chichi did to me in jail. My highly refined palette had been officially destroyed.

Another thing we'd do was take wet chips and boil them. Once they were soft, you molded them into a potato ball. If I used sour cream and onion chips, I could close my eyes and fool myself into thinking I was dining on a baked potato with sour cream and chives.

Well, sort of.

It was a whole new kind of menu in prison. This stuff doesn't come up in Law and Order or Matlock on TV. No, the only way to learn this stuff is to get behind bars. I don't recommend it.

After a few weeks, I started getting regular letters from Ken. Normally, you can't write to other prisoners, because it's too dangerous. They figured it could only cause problems. However, since we had a baby together, we had permission to write back and forth.

Ken would write me a few times a day, all about how we'd be a family on the outside. He'd go off on things that were happening to him, crazy shit that I didn't want to hear about. I wrote him back once a week, just to avoid being completely rude. There was no way I'd ever hook up with him again, but I couldn't tell him that.

He seemed to get the message, though. His letters got belligerent. He accused me of all sorts of things because I wasn't writing more often. He hated that I turned our baby over to Georgia. He blasted me that I was conspiring to keep the baby from him. He wasn't too far off. Pretty soon, I stopped writing and just threw away all his ranting. No point in reading them. It worried me though. He was due to get out before me.

After a week or so, I got a visit from my mother and Cain. Mom did her best to put a smile on her face, but I wasn't fooled.

"You look good," she said.

I laughed. "That's nice of you to say. It's good to see you."

Cain didn't seem too phased by it all. "I love you, Mom," he said.

I fought back the tears. "I love you so much!"

It was bittersweet seeing them. I loved the time together, but got so depressed right after, when they left. One of the perks of being at County was that I was still close by for Mom, so she could come visit.

Since I was pregnant, I was allowed out with Officer Rosie for my prenatal exams. She was nice to me. It was such a luxury getting in a car with her, looking around, being outside. Getting to see things like trees and houses made me realize how much I loved Reading. It took getting locked up to make me really appreciate what I had all my life.

I'd fantasize about hitchhiking down the road, going anywhere, seeing people, just living a life outside prison.

Hell, I'd be okay sleeping on the road, just being out with fresh air and stars above.

But after the hospital visits, I'd be back in the dorm room, eating my potato balls and waiting to go to Muncy State Penitentiary. That was the next step, something I was looking forward to, because it meant I'd be one step closer to getting out.

CHAPTER 9

"Butler!" Officer Louise called out to me. "Time to go!"

It was still dark. I looked over at the clock next to my bed. Four in the morning. My adrenaline was pumping. I wanted to go. I was ready. I wanted to get started with the whole thing, which meant getting on the bus to Muncy State.

Here at County, I was stuck in the big dorm room for twenty-three hours a day. Upstate I'd be able to move around, and more importantly, go outside. Missy explained the whole thing to me. Muncy Prison was like a little city. You eat in one place, go to medical in another, and sleep in another. Eventually, I'd be able to work and maybe get some training. I'd be doing something. I was actually excited.

It had taken County two months to gather ten people that needed to go to Muncy. As we marched out to the bus, everyone else was shackled except for me. Since I was six months pregnant, they let me walk free. Guess they didn't want a lawsuit if I tripped and fell and lost my baby.

The guards always seemed to take good care of me. I was the property of the state. There was no doubt about that. But my miracle baby wasn't. She still had rights, thank the Lord.

The bus ride took three hours. I looked out the window and ate up the outside world. I loved looking at families, kids, and especially old people. Old people rock.

I felt a hand touch my belly. Turning, I looked into the pale blue eyes of the girl sitting next to me. She had stringy blond hair and a bad case of acne.

"What's it like?" she whispered.

"Being pregnant?" I asked.

"Yeah."

"It's great," I said. I loved the feeling, even in these conditions. "There's nothing like having life within you."

"Is it a boy or a girl?"

"A girl."

"She's free," the girl whispered. Her voice held a certain reverence.

"Yeah," I said, rubbing my tummy. "Not like her mommy."

She was quiet the rest of the trip, looking straight ahead. I looked over at her as we approached the gates to Muncy. Her eyes were wide, staring. I squeezed her arm. "Don't worry, it'll be okay."

As we got off the bus, three different girls whispered, "I'm sticking with you, Stacy."

"What?" I said. "Don't do that. I don't know what's going on."

I wondered briefly why these girls thought I was the one to follow. Maybe it had something to do with my faith in God. I wasn't afraid. I think that set me apart from the others. Well, that and being pregnant.

"Stacy," Missy had told me two weeks ago. "You want to get transferred to Cambridge."

"Why?"

"It's minimal security. Muncy's max," she explained. "You need to start at Muncy, but trust me, you don't want to stay there any longer than you have to."

"Okay," I said. "What do I do to get to Cambridge?"

"Behave," she said. "You'll do fine. Just know that's where you want to end up and it will work out."

When we arrived, we all had to go through a classification phase. We were searched again, thoroughly, photographed, and fingerprinted. It wasn't exactly like the quarantine at Berks, thank God, but it was similar. First thing, we had to get cleared medically. They called it med locks. We all needed physicals and another TB shot.

Muncy was all about levels. If you were a murderer, you'd be Level 4. If you screwed up, you'd go to the Restricted Housing Unit (RHU) then you'd be Level 5. All Level 3s stayed at Muncy, but were considered medium security. By the time you got to Level 2, you were eligible for places like Cambridge. That happened when you got points for good behavior. As it turned out, I started at Level 1, because I was a first-time offender.

All the newbies wore blue to set them apart from everyone else. We all referred to it as "the blues." Since I was really suffering, I felt the name was apt. I spent a lot of time trying not to freak out that I was upstate, in jail, far away from my family.

"Stacy," Missy had warned me. "There's no touching, ever. Contact isn't allowed at all. And your family won't be visiting you every week anymore. Things will change."

The other girls all got put in the RHU, the hole, until their medical clearance came. They probably had two girls to a cell. Since I was pregnant, they put me in the infirmary. You'd think this would be better, but in the end, I wished I'd been able to go to the hole.

The infirmary was about a hundred years old, painted an institutional green, like some B-rated horror film. All the doors were double locked and the place was filled with old, senile women who'd been in jail forever. They'd scream day and night, crying loudly.

I was stuck in that hell hole for four days. I had a tiny pencil, three sheets of lined paper and a Bible. There were no hygiene products, so I stunk to high heaven. Well, they did give me a nub of a deodorant stick and scentless soap, but it didn't do much. They let me shower once during the entire time.

During the day, they'd keep the door open in the infirmary. There were prisoners who worked there. That was a huge privilege for them. Those girls would give me extra food and ask to touch my belly a lot. I ended up getting close to a few of them.

Finally, I was released from the infirmary and put in general population on J-Block. I arrived before my roommate and did my best to settle in. I wondered who my celly would be.

When she came in sporting a full beard, it scared the shit out of me. I'd heard that some women took hormones before they came to prison, so they'd look like that. To make matters worse, I soon found out that she'd been in the hole for getting in a fight with someone. Not the greatest recommendation in the world.

When she walked in, she had a huge bag of commissary food. To get commissary food, you had to put in an order the week before. When you first arrive, you can't put in for commissary for a week, so it'd be two weeks before I could receive an order. I was always hungry, so it really sucked.

I'd eat pretty much whatever I was given. I was that starved, eating for two and all. The only exception was this one time, when I found a cockroach in my biscuit. I wasn't hungry enough to eat that, but I managed to swallow the rest of the food, though it wasn't easy.

I read through the Inmate Handbook a few times and learned about something called "Count Time." Still, I wasn't at all prepared when it happened. I was resting on my bed when suddenly an officer boomed out, "It's count time! Cooouuunt tiiiiiime!"

When they call Count Time, you had to stand perfectly still by the door, so that you could be easily counted. It happened a few times a day. You weren't supposed to move, talk, or even go to the bathroom during Count Time. If you did anything but stand motionless, you could be written up. Not what I wanted if I wanted to go to Cambridge.

Sometimes, it would last only fifteen minutes, but if they screwed up the count, it'd be more like an hour. If I was caught in medical during Count Time, I had to sit there on a hard bench.

On the positive side, I did make a number of friends. Some of the girls lived on the top floor, though, which kind of sucked because I wasn't allowed upstairs. It was too dangerous, as inmates would run up and down all the time.

I was also told to take the bottom bunk, so that I couldn't fall by accident. The mattress was about an inch thick, and narrow, smaller than a twin bed. I barely fit. My cellmate's bottom nearly sank to the level of my face. But I got used to it.

We were given supplies to clean the cells twice a day. They needed it, they stunk. I'd usually wake up to the smell of my roommate's shit, just feet from my face. We'd eat breakfast in there, too, which was something I never got used to.

My second day, a girl next to me, yelled, "Yo, Prego, when they pop the lock, make sure you keep your door wide open." Popping the lock is when they open all the doors to the cells at the same time. It's damn loud.

A prickly pain of fear shot through my entire body. I didn't want trouble. Shit, I was so vulnerable with my big belly.

Oh my God! What the hell am I going to do?

I glanced over at my bearded celly with a silent plea for help in my eyes. She shrugged and mouthed, "I have no fucking idea."

If I wanted to go to Cambridge Springs, I needed to keep completely clean and fight free. That was my whole goal now, to make it out of Muncy and into a minimum security place.

If this girl came at me, I'd have to defend myself and my baby. Hopefully, they'd understand it was self-defense. Would my hormone-enhanced celly come to my rescue?

The lock popped with a loud bang and I waited for half a second. My heart stopped beating as I held my breath. I tried not to panic, but failed.

Oh my God, she's coming to get me!

Suddenly, this big bag of food came flying through my door. Turned out, she'd been in the hole for three weeks and had accumulated a bunch of commissary. She was just looking out for me and my baby. I breathed again and thanked her, feeling a little silly.

I was new and pregnant, so I was a person of interest. It's not like that girl and I ever became friends or anything. She was just being generous. It happened now and then in prison.

When I could finally get commissary, I tried to save my food as much as possible. I'd only eat a small bowl of potato chips at a time. Of course, other girls were hungry and if they asked for some, I couldn't say no. I didn't want to be stingy, but I really wanted to keep my food for later.

I'd order lots of tuna packets. And instead of bread, they'd give you tortillas. They lasted longer in the heat. I'd get mayo packets and make wraps. Then I'd buy Ramon noodles and make a sort of tuna casserole. I'd make chichi soup, too, just like Missy taught me. I had some variety going. Sometimes, I could get packets or sticks of chicken or beef and make a little hot meal.

I started making friends with people in the kitchen. They'd steal stuff and sneak it to me. Everyone really went out of their way to help me because of my little daughter growing inside me.

How are things going to change when my miracle baby is born?

After I was acclimated a bit, I could order luxury items, like a TV. Normally, inmates had to wait until they were out of the blues before they got something like that. They just couldn't afford it. However, my sponsor from the recovery program I was in had money and I'd stayed clean and sober, so she sent me hundreds of dollars to buy a TV.

Things in the commissary always cost way more than they did on the street. For instance, the super-small TV I got would run sixty dollars or so on the outside, but in prison the price was three hundred bucks. That's just the way it was. The little TV was see-through, so that you couldn't possibly hide anything inside it. And it was engraved with my ID number on it.

That little TV was a lifesaver. Since it was about a hundred degrees outside, and I was in my third trimester, going out into the yard wasn't any fun. The only thing I really felt like was sitting there and watching my little TV all day.

I'd lie on my bed and prop up the TV so my celly could watch with me. I paid another twenty dollars a month for cable. I loved Turner Classic Movies the best, the old black and white ones about royalty, or PBS, anything that took me out of this horrible world of institutional gray.

☙❧

A few weeks before I was to deliver, they moved me to the infirmary. The last thing anyone wanted was for me to suddenly break my water and deliver in the cell block without any medical attention. I'd made several friends, people I'd grown to like, so it was tough to leave them all in order to go live by myself in the solitary confinement of the infirmary.

The doctor had explained to me that the only real option was a C-section. That's how I had Cain and it was too risky to have a V-BAC, not to mention a surprise delivery date. They kept the scheduled date confidential for obvious security reasons. They were worried that someone could break me out when I went to the hospital.

It was late in the evening of August 23rd when someone banged on my door and yelled, "Ms. Butler! Don't eat anything after midnight!"

"Why?" I asked, already knowing the answer.

The officer chuckled. "Why do you think?"

"I'm having my baby tomorrow!" I squealed with joy.

I jumped up and took a shower. It felt like I'd just gone into labor. I started crying hysterically as I realized that by this time the next day, my miracle baby would be in my arms. I'd get to hold her, smell the top of her sweet head, kiss her cheeks.

Then it hit me.

She'd be out of my body for good. My lifeline to the real world was about to be ripped out of me. I'd be alone after that.

I suddenly freaked, banging hard on the door. "Let me out! Let me out!" I couldn't stand being locked in that room by myself anymore. No one paid any attention.

It was something like four in the morning when they let me out of the cell. "I'm in so much pain!" I cried.

"It'll be okay," the lady officer said. "We're calling the ambulance. Just try to calm down."

I was taken to Geisinger Hospital, which is one of the best hospitals in the US. When I got there, the first thing I noticed was that a lot of normal people were walking around, without shackles, dressed in street clothes. It looked weird to me, coming straight from prison. And here I was, a huge pregnant woman in prison blues being wheeled around in cuffs. I didn't look anyone in the eye.

When I got to my room, I couldn't believe how amazing it was. The bed actually had a headboard and a real mattress, thick and wide. It even had a window that bowed out, so I could stand there and feel like I was outside. It was incredible.

I was supposed to deliver at eleven, but they kept bumping me. Being that I was a prisoner, I was low priority.

Fine with me!

I could chill in that bed and look out the window of my luxury suite forever. The only drawback was that I was starving and I wasn't allowed a bite of food. You can't eat before surgery.

Sometime mid-afternoon, the lady officer assigned to me said, "Ms. Butler, we're going to take you now."

Oh my God!

I was still shackled to the bed as they wheeled me out for surgery. When I got to the operating room, the doctor frowned. "Is it really necessary to keep her chained up during this procedure?"

"Yeah, it is," the officer said.

"Like hell it is," he said, shaking his head. "I'm the doctor here and I'm asking you to take them off immediately. I can't operate like this. It isn't safe."

They complied. I mean, really, was I going anywhere? It wasn't physically possible.

After the spinal, everything went hazy. It all looked so foreign. I didn't know anyone, except the lady correction officer. I liked her, but she was in uniform, in my delivery room.

This is so wrong!

Where was my mother? Where was my sister? I missed them both so much. They'd both been there when Cain was born.

Now, I'm a very spiritual person, but I don't really read the *Bible* much and really don't talk scripture, but suddenly the 23rd Psalm tumbled out of my mouth. "The Lord is my Shepherd. I shall not want. He maketh me to lie down in green pastures."

I felt better. I then went into the serenity prayer and had this overwhelming sense of peace.

Melissa was born a few moments later. She was white with dark, dark hair. And her eyes were big, black, and beautiful. The most beautiful I'd ever seen.

"Is everything okay?" I asked the doctor.

"Yes, everything's just fine," the doctor said.

He told me that he was putting something in the IV to put me to sleep. When I woke up, my little girl was right there in the room with me.

The pain was excruciating, I was so sore. On top of that, I was starved and back in chains. When I had to pee, I had to hold my stomach and walk in shackles. They'd unchain my hands to go to the bathroom, but not my feet.

Despite all that, I did enjoy eating whatever I wanted, as much as I wanted. That's the way it is when you're a patient at the hospital. I kept ordering food all night. It was like Thanksgiving. Turkey sandwiches, chocolate pudding, and vanilla ice cream.

I slept with Melissa in my bed that night. I wasn't supposed to, but I couldn't bear being without her. I changed her diapers as often as possible. I just wanted to make up for all the times I wouldn't get to change her.

In the morning, the phone rang. "Ms. Butler, would you like breakfast?" the cheerful voice on the other end asked.

"Of course, I'll have one of everything!"

She laughed. "Coming right up!"

I called my mom to let her know that I had delivered. Because of the prison regulations, I couldn't call her until the last minute, which was really rough on her. She and Georgia didn't have much time to plan, since they'd have to come all the way upstate to pick up my baby.

"I hope I can make it, Stacy," she told me. "I'll come after work, but it's a three-hour drive."

Georgia didn't drive, so it was all on Mom, as usual. She always seemed to carry the burden of responsibility.

Four o'clock rolled around and nobody was there. I looked at the clock every two minutes.

Come on, Mom!

Finally, the lady officer came up to the bed. "Ms. Butler, we're going to have to take you back now."

"What?" I cried, clutching Melissa to my breast. "What do you mean?"

"We have to go."

"But we can't just leave my baby here. How can I go now? My mom's not here yet."

"You're just going to have to leave her," she said firmly. "If your mom doesn't pick her up within twenty-four hours, the baby will be put into state custody."

CHAPTER 10

After all that, my baby might land in state custody? My body began to tremble uncontrollably. I never felt so helpless.

"Please, just give them a little more time," I said. "I know they'll be here. Please don't ask me to leave my baby girl all alone."

Oh God, please help me.

"There's nothing I can do," she said.

"Please," was all I could say. "Please?"

"Officer Wilkenson," her radio blared. "Come in, please."

"I'm here," she said, her eyes still on me. I held her gaze and my breath.

Please God!

"Muncy's in lockdown. Do you copy?"

Oh my God, lockdown?

The officer looked at me with a smile. "I copy," she said. "I'll hold Ms. Butler here until further orders, over and out."

I shouted for joy and kissed Melissa a thousand times. When the prison is in lockdown, no one can go in or out, which meant I could stay. Actually, it meant I had to stay. There was nowhere else to go.

Thank you, Lord!

My mom and Georgia showed up two hours later. The officer let me visit with them a bit, which was wonderful. I got to see my mom rock Melissa, cooing to her gently. I recorded the memory in my mind, knowing it would be all I'd have for years to come.

At one point, I had to pee. While in bed, I had covered my legs with a blanket, so Mom wouldn't see the shackles, but now I couldn't keep them hidden. She looked away quickly, but not before I saw the look of utter devastation and disgust in her eyes. What mother wants to see her daughter in chains?

Mom and Georgia trundled my baby into a snowsuit and put her in the car seat they'd brought. They both gave me a brief hug before taking her out of the room. The moment they left, I dissolved into tears. It was all wrong.

It's my baby!

I couldn't believe she was gone. Suddenly, the ray of light that had lived with me for so long was gone.

The lockdown lifted at ten that night. I changed back into my blue jumpsuit and they put all the chains on me. I was no longer pregnant, so they shackled my feet, my arms and put chains around my waist, right where I'd had the C-section.

I was taken out by wheelchair to the van. I looked at the van and wondered how I'd climb up. "I can't climb up like that," I said miserably.

The officer put a stool down so I could kneel on it and crawl into the van. My whole body screamed with pain. Normally, a new mother would be resting in the hospital bed, holding her baby. It was the most wonderful time. But here I was, struggling to get into the van that would take me back to jail.

To make matters worse, the ride to Muncy was horribly bumpy and long. By the time I got there, I was in so much pain, I nearly vomited. They brought me straight to the infirmary and let me call Mom.

"I made it back," I told her.

"Good for you," she gritted out.

"Mom, don't be like that."

"What do you expect? You made this mess, Stacy."

"I know."

"This is all your doing."

"Please, I don't have much time," I said. "I just needed to ask that whatever happens, don't let my baby call Georgia 'Mommy,' okay? Just promise me that."

"Give me a break!"

"Mom!" I cried out.

She let out a bitter laugh. "Oh, and how am I supposed to control that?"

"Mom, please!" I was crying so hard by now, I was hiccupping madly. "Please. You're my only hope."

"Go to bed," she said, her voice firm, but motherly. "It's late. You're lucky to have Georgia. Quit whining."

"I know, I know, but you've got to promise me. I don't want Melissa growing up not knowing who her mommy is."

"You should have thought of that when you were dealing drugs and whoring out your friends." The phone clicked and all I was left with was a dial tone.

She's right.

The next day, everything was back to normal, like nothing had happened. The difference was that I no longer carried my baby. I had to walk to meals like everyone else, despite just having had a C-section three days before. I was just like everyone else there, property of the state.

That week, I got my first piece of "Legal Mail." Legal mail is announced separately from regular mail, and you have to sign for it. Anyone on the inside getting legal mail knows to expect horrible news. It's what you get when you've lost a custody battle or you've just gotten the death penalty. However, my letter was different. It could only be one thing—my appeal.

My hands shook as I opened the letter.

Please, God! Please, God!

This could be the answer to all my prayers. I opened the letter and quickly scanned it.

DENIED!

I should have expected it. What else would they say? It's just that when you're in prison, all you have is hope. You actually begin to believe that the impossible might happen.

Now more than ever, I wanted to go to Cambridge Springs. However, I needed to be medically cleared to leave, which meant the stitches had to heal. In the end, it took a month. That period was the worst. Everything, including every twinge of pain, reminded me of having Melissa in my tummy. I was sick of being there without my baby.

My milk came in within a few days. All I wanted to do was nurse my baby. She'd never get that and my milk would just dry up, unused.

Was Georgia feeding my baby enough?

After I gave birth, all calls from Georgia stopped. Somehow I had thought, I'd assumed, I'd be getting tons of photos and phone calls. I longed to hear the gurgles of my little girl, but Georgia went silent. She didn't want to have anything to do with me anymore. Georgia had been a strong supporter for me at the trial and now she just disappeared with my baby.

My mom continued to be pissed at me. Cain was acting up. No one came to visit me. I never felt so alone, so far away from my family. I found myself just counting the days.

When the transfer came through, my energy came back. I was one more step toward getting out.

I loved the ride up. It was invigorating. Cambridge reminded me a bit of the overflow in the county prison, but nicer. There were no doors or locks and no bars on the windows. It was kind of like a college dorm room. They even had curtains on the windows.

I finally got out of the blue prison uniform. I was done with the Muncy blues. My new color was brown. Fine by me. I was desperate to work at Cambridge, but the rule was that you had to wait four weeks before you could get a job.

So I rested for a month, waiting for my opportunity. It was boring, but not intolerable. I could handle four weeks. Still, I nearly jumped for joy when the paperwork came through for me to work in the kitchen.

When I went to orientation in the staff dining room, I sighed with pleasure, looking around at the room.

I could get used to this.

They had a real salad bar, something I hadn't seen in months. And bagels! It was real food. I made an instant decision to find a way to work in that dining room.

I was assigned veggie prep as my first job. Obviously, they weren't about to just give us knives, considering we were all convicted felons. So their solution was to lock us all together in a cage and tie the knives to the cutting boards.

Great, I'm stuck in a confined space with prisoners who have probably killed people with knives!

I just did my best to not make waves, keep my head down, and work. Those knives were so dull, it wasn't easy, but I was determined to do a good job and move up the ladder.

One of the women I got to know was Thelma, who had the nickname of the "polite bank robber," because she used good manners when holding up stores. She was a tall, white woman with long blond hair. She told me she'd always apologize for her crime whenever she robbed anyone. She was a sweet lady and well respected, so she had the privilege to work in the staff dining room.

"It must be nice working there," I said. *Is my envy showing?*

She smiled at me. "Yeah, it's great!"

Not wanting to beat around the bush, I asked, "Any idea on how I could get transferred?"

Thelma nodded. "Actually, we are losing a girl. She's getting paroled in a week."

"Wow, that's great! Any chance you could put in a good word for me?"

She nodded. "Why not?"

Soon after, I had the opportunity to meet with the person who ran that section. I sold myself like I'd never done before. I told her all about my years of working in the restaurant business, promising her that I'd work my ass off. I knew if I was given a chance, I could make the officers very happy. Within two weeks of working veggie prep, I was transferred into the staff dining room. That had to be a record of some kind. I didn't even have to formally apply. I just kissed the right asses and got in. That—and my history of non-violence probably didn't hurt.

One of the biggest perks of working in staff dining was that I could eat anything I wanted. It was a luxury I didn't expect. I could scramble myself eggs for breakfast, pour myself orange juice, and raid the salad bar whenever I wanted. Plus, they had a soda machine. No one in that prison ate better than me.

One of the first things I noticed was the waste. Food was routinely thrown out. When I saw that pans and pans of perfectly good french toast were getting tossed every day, I asked the head cook if I could use them.

She shrugged. "Sure. Why?"

"I make the best bread pudding!" I said.

I wasn't exaggerating, I really did. And true to my word, they all loved it. I kept that job for two years.

I had it good, but regardless of how nice things got, it was still a prison. I had no rights, no freedom. Looking at the same walls day after day could make me sick to my stomach if I let it. I had to focus on my goal of getting out. I couldn't imagine being a lifer. They'd never know anything outside this community. When I felt depressed, I reminded myself I wasn't them.

Once in a while, I'd forget where I was, just for a moment. I'd allow myself to let loose and get caught up with the other women, laughing and talking. It wouldn't last long, though. Soon, it would hit me like an avalanche. My mother, son, and baby girl were all going through hell because of me.

I have no fucking right to laugh.

I made a point of never looking at a sunrise. I knew they were gorgeous, out over Erie, Pennsylvania, but I never wanted to see that beauty. I didn't deserve it. Leave that for the people who didn't disappoint those who loved them.

"You can't keep beating yourself up," a lifer friend, Megan, used to scold me.

"Who am I to enjoy anything?" I'd grumble.

She'd shrug. "You're doing your time."

"Yeah, but my mom's back at home, crying her eyes out. My son is suffering without me, and Melissa," I choked back tears. "Melissa doesn't even know who I am."

"She will," Megan said. "And before you know it, you'll be out."

"Yeah."

"Look," she said. "You're going to have to learn to accept things and do the best you can with whatever happens. You've got to learn to forgive yourself."

"Maybe someday, just not today," I said.

I continued to work in the staff dining room. I got thirty-two cents an hour for my work there. That may sound low to someone who works on the outside, but in prison that's top pay. I had been getting eighteen cents an hour at veggie prep, so I was thrilled with the pay raise.

My sponsors hadn't sent money in months and I was desperate for things. Everything in prison was so expensive. My sneakers cost fifty dollars and a sweat suit was forty. A bar of good soap was a small fortune.

I have to get my hands on some money.

Desperate, I did something stupid, really stupid, which could have gotten me in big trouble. I stole sugar packets from staff dining, concealing them in the soles of my shoes. Sugar was incredibly valuable in the prison, so I could barter with it, get things I wanted. However, if they'd caught me, I would have lost everything. The punishments were severe. I got lucky, though, and never got caught.

Before long, my sponsors, Kim and Cliff, started coming around more. They were married and very devoted to helping me stay sober. I worked out a deal with them where they would send me a hundred bucks a month. I promised to pay them back with the first money I earned when I was released. That was enough money to get what I needed.

After six months, I went to the unit manager and requested to be moved into the B unit, known as the Honor Unit. Since I had a blemish-free record and a good reputation at my job, I was awarded the transfer.

The Honor Unit was an amazing place to be. The rooms were humongous. The only downside was that I had to share the room with five other people. It wasn't a big deal though. The room had a private bathroom with a glorious bathtub. It was like having a luxury suite at a five-star hotel.

We also had two gyms and a flat-screen TV with movie-theater seating. There were DVDs you could check out, too. And the rules were more flexible. For instance, we were allowed to eat in our rooms and there were two microwaves we could use any time.

When I moved up to Cambridge, my mom let me know she wouldn't be able to visit me any longer. That meant I couldn't see my children. The drive was a good six and a half hours, so it just wasn't going to happen. I walked around in a fog, thinking about what it might be like to hold and kiss Melissa and Cain.

Mom knew how much it was killing me, so she promised to work out a visit on my birthday, June 22, 2008. She said she'd bring my sister and her two children as well. It was too many people for her car, so she had to rent a van. They also needed to stay over at a hotel, so the whole trip cost her about a grand.

Mom, you always come through for me. Thank you!

As the big day approached, I became a nervous wreck. It was all I could think of, day and night. Finally, the day before, I was a jittery mess. My hands shook as I prepared the food. Bursts of adrenaline raced through my system every time I thought about how I'd actually get to hold my daughter and hug my son.

A friend in the Honor Unit, who had taken some cosmetology classes at Cambridge, offered to do my hair. It was relaxing, pampering. We weren't allowed scissors, so my friend had to sneak them in. She cut my hair off-camera somehow and put it in rollers wet. Then, in the morning, she took the rollers out and wrapped it again. When she took them back out, my hair was just flowing beautifully. I felt like a human being, a real woman, for the first time in a long while. I could hold my head high.

I wasn't sure when my family would arrive, but visiting hours started at nine. I figured they wouldn't be there that early, being that they would have had to leave Reading at two in the morning. Still, I knew my mom would be there as soon as humanly possible.

I went to the dining room and worked as usual, pretending to go on with my routine as if it were a normal day. What else could I do? I carefully put on my hair net and tried to keep my cool. My bosses were understanding and supportive.

Finally, one of my bosses came up to me and said, "They're here!"

A squeal escaped me. "Oh my God!"

As I took the long walk to the visiting room, my legs felt like they were suddenly made out of rubber. I was steps away from the moment I'd dreamed about for months.

A few more steps and I can hold my children.

I couldn't believe that I was going to be able to *touch* my family.

When I arrived in the adjoining room, I had to do a cavity and strip search. Luckily, I knew the lady officer well, so the horrible, degrading experience was a little less awkward.

She peeked out to the visiting room. "Your family is all out there!"

That burst of adrenaline hit me again. "Do you see them?" I asked.

"I do!"

I felt nauseated. "Did you see a baby?"

"Yeah, there's a little girl, who looks to be about one. Is that her, Stacy? Is that your baby?"

"Yeah, that's my baby! Do you see a big boy, too?"

"Yup, he's there. Cain, right?"

I felt relief. They were all here. "Yeah, that's right. He has Asperger's, you know."

The officer was finishing up her search. "You know, I have a nephew with Asperger's."

I looked at her. "Really? I didn't know!"

"Yeah, it's a challenge, I can tell you that, but I love him."

"They are such a blessing," I said.

When she finished the search, I had to change back into the nasty brown one-piece jumpsuit. At least my hair looked good!

When I came out, the first thing I noticed was that my sister, Megan, was furious.

I learned later that the officer who let the visitors in that day was the one guard who hated me. She had a militant personality. Her viewpoint was that no inmate should ever have any privileges. So you can imagine that she resented the hell out of me. She gave my family a rough time.

My mom looked completely disheveled, like she'd just been through a storm. Cain looked bewildered. He was holding my little girl. The first person to actually greet me was my nephew, Amir.

"Aunt, Stacy!" he cried, leaping into my arms. "I love you!"

I hugged him tightly. "I love you, too!"

I looked over at my mom. "Hello!"

"Hi," she said, giving me a stiff hug.

"How was the drive up here?"

"Don't ask," she grunted.

I realized that she probably had about four hours of sleep the night before and the kids had most likely been misbehaving the entire trip. Then they arrived to find a vindictive guard, who was bent on ruining this special day for me. It was a little too much for all of them.

Looking at Melissa, drinking up everything about her, I quickly saw that she had no idea who I was.

"I'm your mommy!" I said with a big smile.

She shook her head and looked away. That single action confirmed my worst fears. Georgia hadn't followed my pleas to make sure my baby knew I was her true mommy. To Melissa, Georgia was mommy, not me.

I bit back tears. I couldn't let her see my devastation. I couldn't let Georgia ruin this day for me.

"Sweetie," I said patiently. "I'm your mommy. Come here and give me a hug."

She looked back at me, hesitated for a moment and then came into my arms. I felt an overwhelming sense of relief. My little girl relaxed into me as if she somehow remembered that she had just come out of my body a year ago. She knew.

I held Melissa tightly, while I chatted with my mother and sister. Cain sat quietly in a chair nearby. We talked about the weather, the happenings of Reading and other mundane topics, safe subjects, boring things.

When Melissa fell asleep on my chest, it felt like the crazy world had righted itself for that moment. Time ticked away by the beats of her little heart. I was her mother. And she was still my baby girl. Her tiny chest rose and fell in perfect rhythm. I relished each of her little breaths as they caressed my neck.

If only this moment could last a lifetime.

We took many pictures throughout the visit. It was wonderful to have them all. When Melissa woke up, we all bought snacks from the vending machines. The funny thing was, I think it was equally exciting for me as it was for the kids. It was a little thing we could share and remember.

Each moment I shared with them was heartbreakingly poignant. Unfortunately, the sweeter the moments, the more depressed I became. The clock was my enemy, ticking away the time remaining until they had to leave me again.

"We should go," Mom said after three hours.

"I want to go in the pool!" Cain shouted.

Guess I'm the secondary attraction here.

Yes, I was jealous, but I couldn't blame him. Kids love hotel pools.

"Go have fun," I told him.

"We'll be back tomorrow," Mom promised.

"I can't wait!" I did my best to hide the desperation that threatened to swallow me. Did they see the dense cloud that seemed to surround me?

The next day, my family spent another four hours with me. I didn't want to hurt, to feel the incredible loss that would come from saying goodbye to my children again, so I separated myself from everything. I adopted a jovial attitude, one that everyone could feel comfortable around. This would be the last visit until I was released. I needed to make it perfect.

I watched them leave. Despite the instant depression I felt, I realized I was now newly energized to do what I needed to do. I redoubled my efforts to get out early.

CHAPTER 11

As I sautéed carrots and put water on to boil for the rice for dinner prep, I realized that if I wanted to go home sooner, I needed to aggressively pursue Therapeutic Community, T.C. for short, a pre-release program for drug users. I wouldn't need to take violence prevention courses or sexual offender classes, because they didn't apply to me. I was lucky that with my good record I could be productive and not wallow in depression. It would have been a nightmare to sit in a cell all day.

T.C. lasted six months and was a necessary step in order to be allowed to leave prison early. Typically, you could only hope to leave a year before your sentence was up, if you were approved for probation. Since I still had two years to go, it would be a bit unheard of for me to enter the program. The waiting list was over a year long.

I saw Thelma and waved her over. She asked about the family visit and I put on a cheery smile, chatting about all the nice points.

I didn't mention the gaping hole in my heart.

When I had given her all the details, I paused and asked, "Do you know who works D Block?"

D Block was where the T.C. prisoners were housed. I would need to give up the frills of the Honor Unit, but I didn't care. I wasn't in prison to have a good time. I needed out, now!

"Sure, there's Mary and Jo Beth," she said, indicating two large black ladies sitting together. I'd been serving them all this time and didn't even know.

I nodded. "Anyone else?"

Thelma looked around the room. Her eyes lit up. "Why, there's Mr. McClary. He's the nicest guy you'll ever meet."

"Thanks," I said, looking over at him.

He was a tall, thin, white man with wire-rimmed glasses. He wore a gray vest and burgundy bow tie.

I brought Mr. McClary extra food and introduced myself. He smiled and thanked me. I also brought extras to Mary and Jo Beth, who smiled. Overall, the staff appreciated my efforts. The fact was that many of the staff wouldn't eat unless I was cooking for them. They just didn't trust anyone else with their food. If I wasn't working, they'd eat from the vending machines.

After about a week, I took the next step. I checked myself briefly in the mirror, tucking away stray strands of hair here and there. Then I took a deep breath and approached Mr. McClary.

"I really want to go to T.C.," I told him after our usual chit chat. *Okay, subtlety was never my strong suit.*

He laughed. "Direct, aren't you?"

"Yes, sir," I said.

"How much time do you have left?"

"Two years," I answered. "But you need me there. I can help. I've been sober three years and two months."

He took a bite of my chicken parmesan and said, "I'll look over your file."

"I'm not sure my file is complete," I said.

"Oh?"

"It probably doesn't show that I worked steps with women at the recovery house."

He grinned. "You want this bad, don't you?"

"It's just that my children need me," I said. "And I need them."

"We've considered having long-term beds again, so that people like you could come in and help out. I'll see what I can do."

I knew it was a long shot. They never let women enter the program this early. My plan was to get through the program fast and then work there, helping others until I got paroled. And if I played my cards right, I'd be asked to become a peer assistant, which is like a counselor. I needed training, but if I got it, that pay was amazing, and more importantly, it was like a gold star on my record for the parole board.

I kept treating the staff from D Block really well. I didn't push Mr. McClary too much after that initial conversation. He understood how badly I wanted the transfer, so I figured my presence was enough. Sometimes, I talked to him about Melissa and shared with him my worries about how Georgia was bringing her up. He was always a good listener.

One day, I got called to go to D Block. *This is it!* My heart raced as I ran to the building.

An older man greeted me. "Are you ready for T.C.?"

"Yes!" I nearly shouted.

"Mr. McClary asked me to interview you. When would you be ready for the transfer?"

I shrugged. "A few weeks?" That seemed pretty fast.

He laughed. "How about tomorrow?"

"Tomorrow's good," I said without hesitation.

Shit, tomorrow? Really?

I was moved out of the posh Honor Unit into D Block that day. I had to give up my thirty-two cent an hour job at the staff dining hall, with all the perks of extra food, but I didn't care. Moving to T.C. meant moving closer to the day when I could hold Melissa again.

But I'm going to miss the soda machine and all-you-can-eat ice cream.

Going to D Block wasn't an easy transition. Once there, I wouldn't be allowed to talk to anyone who wasn't in the program. No one. All the other inmates were viewed as possible detriments to my recovery. They figured isolating D Block was the only solution. That meant that every single person I'd met in jail up until then was now off-limits.

I knew I'd be tested on a daily basis, as I would probably run into them all the time. I wouldn't be allowed to say a word. They'd probably try to talk to me, but I'd have to ignore them. The only two things that really mattered were Cain and Melissa. I kept my focus on them. My friendships in prison were just temporary.

Before I left, I went back to staff dining and broke the news to everyone. The reaction was pretty uniform. People were encouraging, but jealous as hell.

"When do you go?" Thelma asked.

"Sometime tomorrow," I replied.

"So this is the last time I'll see you then."

I looked at her. "I'll see you, but I just won't be able to do more than nod a hello."

"Not allowed to talk to me anymore?"

"No," I said.

"How did you get in?" she asked. "I mean, there's a huge waiting list. Girls wait years to get there and you're being transferred way before your time."

I shrugged. "Lucky, I guess." I wanted to tell her that she could have done what I did, but I couldn't afford to give away all my secrets. Besides, I didn't think it would work twice. And I wasn't sure Thelma had the drive or determination to get through T.C.

She gave me a quick hug and walked off. No one really talked to me for the rest of the day. They seemed to already consider me part of T.C., getting a head start on the silent treatment.

Better get used to it!

Late that night, I was called and told to pack all my stuff. It didn't take long. Walking into D Block, I sighed. It was like going back eight steps. I'd forgotten how bad general population could smell.

"This is your room," the guard said. I tossed my stuff on the empty cot and looked at my cellies, who were in bed already. It was a few minutes until lights out.

I looked at the big black girl and instantly knew we weren't going to get along.

"That's Trudy," the guard whispered.

I nodded. Trudy had a crazy look in her eye. She just stared at me as I organized my stuff as best I could. The other girl obviously didn't care much for Trudy. She was quietly reading a magazine and ignored me. *Just as well.*

Life on D Block was super-strict and structured. We all woke up together at five forty-five sharp. We had breakfast followed by a community meeting. There were about sixty girls in that building. Every room had three girls. I didn't spend much time in the cell.

After the community meeting, we went to group therapy. I really liked Ms. Willow, the lady that ran our group. She was the DATS, Drug and Alcohol Treatment Specialist. She and my boss, Ms. Bonner, became friends of mine in prison. I trusted them, liked them, and looked up to them. And in turn, they treated me like an equal, something I hadn't experienced since coming to prison.

The first day was rather tame. We had classes, group therapy, food, more group therapy and classes, then dinner. The final meeting was nine at night, signaling the end of the day.

I was there to learn, but everyone knew I was being groomed to be a peer assistant, working side by side with the DATS when I graduated. I didn't get any special treatment because of it, but ran through the program like everyone else.

There was a lot of focus on death. Being that we were all already in jail, the idea was that we only had death left if we screwed up. When someone messed up, we did a mock funeral for them. It was serious. There was a casket and a whole long service with an obituary. It scared the shit out of people.

For me, they had me write obituaries on my kids, because I was always so torn up about them. I cried often and Mr. McClary thought it would help to have me face their death. It wasn't far off for me, actually. My daughter really didn't know that I existed and I never saw Cain. It was almost like they weren't really alive. When I wrote

Melissa's obituary, I realized that she wasn't really dead, but being taken care of. I had to stop feeling so sorry for myself and just get on with it.

Georgia occupied most of my mind. I'd go into internal tirades on that bitch until I made myself sick. Ms. Willow had me write a letter of gratitude to her. It wasn't easy at first, but I found some gratitude for her. I just hated how she deserted me when Melissa was born. Still, she had made a life for my daughter. Melissa was safe.

Many inmates didn't make it through the program. There was no swearing, no inappropriate behavior of any kind, but they allowed you a few slip-ups before kicking you out. Some faked their way through the program, not really doing the steps. I knew who they were. They'd light up a joint the second they got out. It was their choice, but they'd probably wind up back in prison.

While I was in T.C., I got a letter from Ken that made my skin crawl. He was crazier than usual, talking about how I was conspiring with Georgia to keep Melissa from him. He was getting ready to leave prison and was obsessed with my daughter. The last line of his letter seared a hole through my heart.

"I'm going to take the baby to Alaska where you'll never find us!"

Shit, here I was stuck in prison, completely helpless, a property of the state, a nothing. I brought the letter to the captain and asked what I could do. It was a threat and damn if I was going to let a drug addict murderer get ahold of my baby.

In the end, Ken did get in trouble for threatening me, but it didn't affect his release date. He was out in February 2009. All I could do was push on and pray, doing what I could to fight for my baby.

Thank God for Georgia. She was the only thing stopping my lunatic ex-boyfriend from gaining custody of my miracle girl.

When the guard called Legal Mail for me early in March, my blood ran cold. I knew it must be Ken. He was out and was filing for custody of Melissa. All I had was a simple document between me and Georgia, stating that I would keep all rights to my daughter. I had it notarized in prison. It wasn't signed by anyone and therefore probably didn't mean much.

Ken had an attorney and had the advantage of being free, not stuck behind bars like I was. My mother kept up with Georgia, visiting her grandbaby as often as she could. She let me know that Georgia was entertaining Ken on a regular basis.

Shit, Ken was trying to get to Melissa any way he could. I could just see him telling Georgia that they could be a family together, and that together they could take Melissa from me.

Fortunately, it didn't last. Georgia wasn't a stupid woman. Crazy, obsessed with my daughter, maybe, but not dumb. She could see through Ken pretty easily. Their brief honeymoon ended and Georgia and Ken were in a heated battle for the rights to Melissa.

I did everything I could. I wrote letters to Georgia's attorney, asking what I could do. I wrote the judge, asking him to let Melissa stay with Georgia, begging him not to turn over my baby to a homicidal maniac.

All I could do was sit and wait. I must have received something like ten motions from Ken.

I went through T.C., embracing all aspects of the program, doing whatever I needed to do to finish. When I graduated, it was a very proud moment for me. Normally, when you finish the program you go back to a regular block, but I was different. Mr. McClary immediately hired me as a peer assistant, the most honorable job any prisoner could get.

I became a resident of D Block and ran the drug unit. All the same rules applied. I wasn't above that. However, I did have my own office. Plus, I could take out all sorts of media equipment to different parts of the jail, which was unheard of for an inmate.

The former Queen B hasn't lost her touch!

I started out on the third floor, where I'd been when I was going through the program. However, Mr. McClary had other plans for me. He moved me to the first floor immediately, right next to him.

We talked about my forming classes in order to teach the women there. I really wanted to mentor them, help them get to where I was, give them stability. I knew I could make a difference in their lives, give them hope for a future.

Then one day, clear out of the blue, Mr. McClary just keeled over while mowing his lawn. He died instantly of a heart attack. It was like someone had turned the floor on its side and I just tumbled down. I couldn't breathe.

It was the first time I faced death sober. I don't know what I would have done without the training Mr. McClary had given me. It was a real testament to his faith in me that I was able to handle it. We were allowed to have a memorial for him within the walls of the prison. He was beloved by many.

A week or so after the funeral, I found out that Mr. McClary's request for my classes had been approved. He'd submitted it before he passed away. That man was always looking out for me.

I enjoyed those classes. I remember the first day I entered my classroom, I recognized one of the girls from my days as a madam. It stopped me dead in my tracks. It was crazy. One of my whores was there, ready to learn from me. It was like a different lifetime for me. I checked it with the counselor.

"Are you sure I should do this?"

"Stacy, you'll be the best teacher for her. Believe me," she said.

I put together programs based on what Mr. McClary and I had worked on. It was pretty complete and we did them all. The women were grateful, for the most part. Some were fakers, but I didn't judge.

I was also asked to speak to an elementary school. I got into a gray sedan with two other inmates. We didn't talk. We weren't friends. I stared straight ahead, not even looking out the window. It was wrong to enjoy any measure of freedom.

I'm not free. So what if I'm in a car?

It was prison mentality.

The drive took twenty minutes. When I got out, we were escorted directly into the gym. We were wearing our browns, but I was allowed to spend a little time to curl my hair and do a bit of make-up.

The other two girls looked nervous, so I offered to go first. I looked down at my uniform and then looked out at the children. There were about a hundred of them there. They all had on bright colors and different patterns.

I pointed to a boy wearing a red shirt and said, "That's a nice red shirt."

He beamed at me, sitting up straighter. I smiled back.

I then found a girl in a pretty pink dress and said, "That's a cute dress. I like the lace."

I pointed out a few more outfits until the children were all looking around at each other. "You all have such lovely clothes!" I said. "I only have one color. Brown," I told them.

They were hushed, looking at me.

"Did you have Lucky Charms for breakfast this morning?" I asked. "Maybe waffles with maple syrup?" I waited for the children to nod their heads.

"Well, I can't have Lucky Charms," I said. "See, I committed a crime and now I have to pay the consequences. It's kind of like when you do something that your mom told you not to, you know, and then you're not allowed to watch TV. Only it's much worse. Much worse."

I continued to talk to them about how I had to stay in prison for a while because I'd done something against the law. As I looked out, I noticed that none of these little kids were fidgeting or talking. All eyes were on me.

My talk only lasted fifteen minutes. The other girls had trouble following me. Unfortunately, the kids started getting restless. Pretty soon, it was time to go and they all said good-bye to us.

∽∾∽

As the months rolled on, the motions from Ken continued. However, something changed and they were arriving handwritten instead of typed. I found out that he had fired his lawyer and was representing himself. Having been a jailhouse lawyer for years and having the ego he did, he thought he could do it himself.

Ken had been out for six months and I could tell from his handwritten letters that he'd relapsed. It wasn't surprising. It was a pattern with him. He had never lasted more than six month being sober.

I knew the judge was bound to notice the change and guess he was under the influence again. However, Ken was pulling every stall tactic he could come up with to prolong the process. The motions and continuances kept coming. Even though I knew deep down that he couldn't possibly win, I still felt so helpless. He was on the outside, which meant he had so much more power.

One thing that worried me was that Ken managed to complete a child care class that was something like three hours long. For some reason, Georgia failed to attend that class. It ate me up at night.

Would the judge favor Ken?

Mom stayed on top of things, though, looking out for Melissa, like a guardian angel. She helped with attorney fees and did what she could. She didn't want her granddaughter to wind up with Ken any more than I did.

I called Mom regularly, hoping for good news. One day, I got it.

"Stacy, it's over," she said, excitedly. "Ken's nowhere to be found. He didn't show up for court today."

I sighed heavily in relief. "Praise Jesus!"

"You have no more worries," she said. "Melissa's safe with Georgia."

It didn't take long for my gears to switch back to being afraid of Georgia's hold on my daughter.

"Is she calling her 'Mommy?'" I asked.

Mom didn't say anything. I closed my eyes and waited a few moments. When she still didn't respond, I asked, "Mom, please be straight with me. What is my baby calling that woman?"

"What do you think she's calling her, Stacy?" she asked, the steel tone coming back into her voice.

I could tell that she was losing patience with me, but it was too important. Mom was my only link to the outside world, my only link to my baby. "Do you think that's right?" Tears sprang to my eyes. "It was the one thing I asked of her. It's so important to me."

"Stacy, I'm not getting into this with you. I'm just here to help my grandchild. This whole thing you have with Georgia is the least of my concerns."

I managed to end the phone call politely, but when I hung up, I swore up and down for a minute before I steeled myself again. The rule was that you could apply for Pre-Release a year before your sentence was up. I'd gotten my four-year sentence on April 20, 2007, so theoretically, I might have been able to leave April 20, 2010. That was the absolute earliest possible release date.

And that was the absolute latest I'd tolerate.

In order to be released, I needed a hearing with the board. They wanted to see change, improvement. They asked a lot of questions about what I was going to do when I got out and how I was going to apply what I'd learned. They wanted to see that I'd actually contribute to society, instead of being the drain on it that I had been.

In January 2010, I was called down to the guidance office. This was two years and eight months into my sentence.

The lady looked at my sympathetically. "Please have a seat."

Uh oh! That doesn't sound good. My mind raced. Something was wrong. I could tell from her expression. *Shit! What happened? Would I have to stay longer?* My heart hammered in my chest. "What's wrong?"

"They only let people out on Mondays," she said.

"Okay..."

"You've been approved for pre-release, but April 20th is a Tuesday."

I digested this news. What was she trying to tell me? "Okay, so what does that mean?"

"You'll have to wait until April 26th to get out."

I relaxed. "That's fine," I said. So it was a week off. I could live with that.

I went back to D Block and waited. I kept up with my routine, but it was getting harder and harder. I tried to keep my release date a secret, but the word got out and people started to avoid me. I wasn't asked to play cards anymore and I found myself alone a lot of the time.

The lifers loved to mess with people whose release date was coming. It was a game they played. It was common to hear, "I'm going to take your fucking date!" I was lucky. I didn't get that shit. I think they knew that if they messed with me, the captain would know. I was so clean, I was almost untouchable. Plus, I was ready to protect my date with my life.

About two months before my release date, I was in the bathroom doing an inspection. It was one of my duties to make sure the place was spotless. It wasn't. The sink in particular was disgusting.

Pissed off, I opened the door and yelled down the hallway, "Whoever's in charge of the bathroom had better get back here on the double. The sink needs to be cleaned *now*!"

One girl glared at me and replied coolly to one of her friends, "She's got a pretty big mouth for someone who's getting ready to leave soon!"

I did my best to mask the jolt of fear that shot up my spine. The last thing I needed was for them to come after me.

The girl responsible for the bathroom came in with her head down and muttered, "Sorry. I'll take care of it."

If she hadn't, I probably would have done it myself. No use in risking a fight. Two more months left, only two months, then, freedom! It didn't seem real.

One day, the captain called me into her office and asked me to sit down. She showed me two disciplinary slips written against me. In prison, it's called "dropping a slip." It's basically snitching.

I read them over. Panic welled up inside me as I realized that this could be the end of my dreams of seeing my children in two months. One slip was from a girl named

Marcy, saying that I had been passing cigarettes. Shit, if they believed her, it would carry a severe penalty. I was a peer assistant and this sort of behavior wasn't tolerated.

I remembered one girl in T.C. was flirting with an inmate, who wasn't in the program. Marcy, another peer assistant, and I had been watching her. It was a flagrant violation, one that probably should have been reported, but I knew the goal of the program was to help those girls.

I turned to Marcy, seeking her advice as she had been a peer assistant far longer than I. "What do you think I should do? How can I help her?"

"Don't bother," she had scoffed. "Write her up!"

I never asked for Marcy's advice again.

The other slip was from Erin. It said, "Stacy Butler was in the bathroom last Tuesday using curse words at another inmate in an intimidating tone." My mind flashed to the incident from three days ago about the sink.

I never cursed.

I knew the rules and always checked every word I uttered. Swearing would get me in tons of trouble. Peer assistants must remain above the rest of the population.

"Captain, I don't know what to tell you," I said, my head hung low.

If she believed any part of either of these complaints, there went my date. I'd be in this hell hole for another six months at least. The captain was a tough disciplinarian.

She didn't put up with anything from anyone. These two lifers knew that.

"Don't worry, Stacy," she said. "I know you and I don't believe either of these two reports for a minute. I'm just showing them to you, because I wanted you to know what was going on."

I sighed in relief. *Thank God!*

"Erin had been my roommate at one point. She never liked me. We used to get into these stupid arguments over space. She didn't want anyone touching her desk or her curtain, the one on what she considered *her* window. I remember when she told me that I would never get custody of my daughter."

The captain put up her hand, effectively stopping me from rambling on and on. "I know Erin and Marcy. You don't need to say anything more. And believe me, I'll make sure they understand I don't appreciate false reports!"

I smiled. "Thank you!"

"Sure," she said. "Now, you want to get out of here, right?"

"Yeah," I said emphatically.

"So what are we going to do about all this? Those two aren't going to let up."

I thought for a moment. "Do you think I fit the criteria for Quehanna Boot Camp?"

"Sure, of course you would. But is that what you really want?" Her doubt showed on her face. It wasn't a request many made. Quehanna was a serious boot camp, in every sense of the term. It was harsh, but it would solve things, get me out of here.

I looked at her hard. "Yes, please put me on the next bus to boot camp, seriously. I have to get out of here because things are getting too crazy."

When I walked out of her office, I felt much better. I knew she'd take care of things. I was safe. I just had to lay low until I could leave. That was Friday afternoon.

As I had hoped, the captain made it happen for me.

The next Monday morning, I was told to pack for Quehanna. The place was located in Elizabethtown, about six hours away by bus. It's up in the hills, in a nice location.

When I arrived, I was put in the barracks with a hundred bunk beds lined up. I wasn't signed up to do the boot camp, but was housed with other girls who were. It was a sweet deal for some inmates who received leniency. They could do the six-month program and go home, rather than serve out their sentence. Some of those girls had been sentenced to four to eight years like me, but got off within six months.

For me, I qualified because there was an overflow in population. Since I was sent to Quehanna, they could send someone else to Cambridge.

I was surprised to find that everyone seemed to expect me just to lie around. I was way too bored. Back at

Cambridge, I was used to working every day. I liked that. I didn't like the idea of being so useless.

I picked up their handbook and saw that they were supposed to have a Therapeutic Community, like that one back at Cambridge. I noticed that they didn't have a peer assistant, which is an essential part of the program so I wrote a letter, asking if I could be the peer assistant for two months. I got a quick reply: "Not interested."

What? Why?

That weekend, the deputy warden came through on a "walk by." I couldn't resist. I just had to talk to her.

"I was trained as a peer assistant back at Cambridge, so I could help out here and be your peer assistant. You currently don't have one, but should. I have two months left on my sentence. I just want to help. When I offered, they said no. Why won't they let me?"

She looked puzzled. "I have no idea, but I'll look into it."

In two days, I had an offer to be the first-ever peer assistant at Quehanna. The pay was fifty-two cents an hour, which is the highest pay I'd ever gotten in jail. I only had two months to create the program, but I threw myself into it. It was much better than lying around all day.

Most of the girls were eager to embrace the program, because we were all on the road home. Quehanna was different from the other prisons. The food was actually good and there were men there, which was a welcomed change. I hadn't seen a man in a while.

I took about twenty girls under my wing, working the program with them diligently. They needed me and I needed to help them. Plus, I was proving to myself that I could make a difference if I put my mind to it.

"If you want to make money on the outside, you have to think outside the box. You have to become an entrepreneur. Push through things that might come up," I told them.

Yolanda, a large black woman with a permanent scowl, folded her arms across her large chest. "That's bullshit."

"Speak your mind, why don't you?" I said.

Her gaze was steady. "No one's going to hire us."

"Not with that attitude. You'll be lucky to wipe tables at Mc D's!"

"It has nothing to do with attitude."

"Yeah," another girl chimed in. "She's right."

"No, she's not," a slender black girl said.

"Teresa, right?" I asked.

"That's right," Teresa said with a nod. "Why don't you two give it up and listen to Ms. Butler? She knows a thing or two."

"Whatever," Yolanda said, shrugging and looking out over my head to the far wall.

I can't reach everyone.

"Look," I said to the other girls. "When you get out, visit me. If you're ambitious enough, you'll find me. I'll help you."

We had a productive two months. I think I may have helped those girls. They told me I had, but it's hard to know if they were just telling me what I wanted to hear.

Soon, I would be released into the halfway home, ADAPPT. I spent a lot of time mentally preparing for life outside prison, figuring out how I would reconcile with my friends and family. Helping the girls at Quehanna gave me the confidence that I deserved another chance.

I wrote a letter to Effie a few weeks before my release, asking for my job back. She had said I could wait tables if I did the right thing, kept clean, and stayed out of trouble. But that was three years ago and I had no idea if she was still at the Charcoal Chef. I poured out my heart in that letter and prayed.

I knew I could get any old job, but being accepted back by Effie, being allowed to work at the place I loved, meant everything to me. I'd get my answer when I arrived at her doorstep.

As it turned out, I was able to go home on April 20, 2010, instead of having to wait until the 26th. Quehanna didn't have the same rules as the other prisons, so they didn't care what day you left. Through God's grace I was able to leave after only serving three years on a four to eight year sentence.

CHAPTER 12

The night before my day of release, I couldn't believe I was actually going home. I think every prisoner goes through that. The system does a final check to make sure there are no outstanding warrants on you. I saw many girls expect to be released only to be put back in the system, answering an old crime. Those girls were expedited back to their county, where they stood trial all over again. Fortunately, I had nothing to worry about.

I knew I needed a ride home. I was only an hour and a half from Reading, but sadly nobody wanted to pick me up. Mom was working, and my sister was done with me. Delores would be my case worker, so she couldn't do it. She wasn't allowed to show any form of favoritism. Fraternization was forbidden.

I contacted a good friend, Julie, who called around for me. It was ridiculous to think that I didn't have a ride home. If I had to, I could have taken the bus, but that was too depressing. Taking the bus meant spending one more night in prison. My stomach churned. I had to get out of there.

Finally, Julie phoned to say that an old friend, Gwen, had offered to help out. Julie apologized to me for not coming herself.

"You have four kids and two jobs. I understand," I said. "I'm just grateful you found someone!"

"Yeah, Gwen was happy to do it," Julie said. "She thinks the world of you."

"That's great," I said. "You have no idea."

"I think I do."

The next day, six in the morning, I shot out of bed and was dressed faster than anyone. I ate my last prison breakfast, I hoped.

Three other random inmates played pinochle with me. I don't remember their names. We played a few hands. Normally, I'd win, but today I played like shit. My hands shook.

"Rides come at eight," one of them said.

"Yeah," I said, staring at the cards in front of me. "It's the longest hour I've ever had to wait."

"If she comes at all," one of the girls at another table called out.

Jealous bitch!

I didn't say anything to her, mostly because she voiced my fear. What if Gwen blew me off? It was a ninety-minute drive. And it was raining. I'm not sure I'd jump out of bed at the crack of dawn to help out a girl I hadn't seen in three years.

I wiped my brow, about to pass four cards when the phone rang. It was eight sharp.

This is it! It's got to be!

I dropped my cards face up. The game was over. My heart stopped as I stared at the guard, who seemed to pick up the phone in slow motion.

"Butler!" she called out with a huge smile. "Get out of here!"

Some fifty inmates all clapped and cheered. One of their own was breaking free. I walked out the door, feeling like I'd just won the Super Bowl.

Rain drizzled on my face. I closed my eyes for a moment and allowed the water to wash over me, cleansing me. The rain was lovely on my face. This was the last walk. I was done.

Thank you, God! Thank you!

I walked into a little room where the papers were processed. The first thing I did was step behind a curtain, a strung-up sheet really, to change into my release clothes. Mom had sent a plain white T-shirt, gray sweats with purple stripes, and butt-ugly, purple Danskin sneakers.

You've got to be kidding me.

It was going to be a while until Mom forgave me. That was clear. She wouldn't have been caught dead in these clothes. She was making a statement. I looked down and grinned. It didn't matter. They were the clothes of a free woman.

Some people didn't have clothes when they walked out. They had to wear oversized clothes donated from a local mission. At least I had something, even if I was wearing grapes on my feet.

I signed a single page, my walking papers. I didn't bother to read it. What choice did I have, right?

When I came out of the room, I saw Gwen. She was an average-sized white girl with a short bob and big smile. I gave her a big hug.

"Thanks, Gwen!" I said, squeezing her hard.

"No sweat," she replied.

"Let's get out of here!"

As we walked to the car, she asked, "You hungry?"

I laughed. "You're kidding, right?"

"I passed this greasy spoon on the way over here."

"Sounds wonderful!" I couldn't remember what it felt like to sit in a restaurant with people who weren't in prison.

I opened the door to her car. Her friend, Niva, was in the backseat. "Hi, Stacy!"

"Hey!"

"Want a smoke?" Gwen asked.

"Do you have one?"

"Sure," she said, pointing to the glove compartment. My hand trembled as I took out a cig.

"How long has it been?" Gwen asked.

"Too long," I said. "Something like two months." I smoked when I could in prison, but Quehanna had strict rules. No smoking allowed. It was rough.

I was just about done with the last drag when we got to the diner. "Bacon," I murmured as we walked up to the door.

Gwen and Niva giggled. We got a booth and I ordered the biggest meal on the menu, fresh OJ, tons of bacon, and three scrambled eggs. Real eggs, not the powdered stuff.

I could only eat half. It was way too much and way too rich. I went to the bathroom and smoked another cig. I needed to pace myself or I'd throw up. My system wasn't used to all this stuff.

It wasn't long before we were headed for ADAPPT, the building I'd call home for the next year.

We passed a Popeye's Chicken and I let out a moan. "Can we stop?"

Gwen squealed the tires for effect, making the U-turn.

I laughed. "Thanks."

I was craving so many things, but that chicken was top on my list. I just had to have some. It had been so long.

"Must be strange," Niva said. She'd been quiet in the back.

"Hmm?" I asked with a mouthful of chicken.

"Well, it's just that you've been cooped up for so long with no say in what you eat or where you go and now, well, you can say, 'Hey, let's stop for some chicken.' It must be a little weird," Niva said.

I stopped eating and wiped my mouth with a napkin. Turning around, I looked Niva in the eye. "To be honest, it doesn't seem too real yet. But I promise you, I'll get used to it fast."

We all laughed. The rest of the drive was uneventful, except that everything I saw looked new and special. Cars, houses, sign posts, all of it. I spent a good hour in silence just smoking and looking around at the world, feeling free again.

We pulled up to the halfway house by early afternoon. "Halfway house" was certainly the right word for the place. It was in-between jail and living free. More like jail, really. ADAPPT had taken over three row homes and converted them into one house. I stared up at the brick building with white trim windows and doors.

Delores came out. I longed to crush her in a bear hug, but it wasn't allowed. Her eyes sparkled, though. That would have to keep me content for the moment.

"Welcome to ADAPPT!" she said, opening the door for me. "Sit here. There's a dozen or so people ahead of you."

I waited for hours before she called me in. She invited me into her office and closed the door.

"I've been hearing good things from the other girls," she said.

"Thank you," I said, looking down at my hands.

She handed me a bunch of paperwork to sign, telling me all the rules. I knew most of them. No smoking in the rooms, no cell phones, and blackout restriction for the first few days. After that period, I'd need to sign out to go anywhere.

"Any infractions could lead to a one-way ticket back to prison," she said sternly.

I nodded. "I understand."

Her voice softened. "I always believed in you."

I looked up, my eyes misted. "Thank you. That means everything to me."

Since I had nothing in the way of possessions, I got the indigent package consisting of shampoo, soap, and other basic toiletries. Delores also handed me linens before directing me to a small room with two bunk beds. Two girls were in there, occupying one of the bunk beds.

Oh, crap! Just my luck!

Nelly, a big black girl, got up and folded her arms across her chest. "If it isn't the big Queen B herself, come to grace us with her presence."

"Shut it," I muttered low. I didn't look at her, but put my stuff on the lower bunk. The room stank of cigarettes.

"This is the girl you were telling me about from Cambridge?" the white girl next to her said.

"That's right," Nelly answered her.

"She thinks she's hot shit, doesn't she?" the other girl said.

Nelly nodded. "Look, *Ms. Butler*, things are different here."

"How about you just leave me alone?" I walked out of the room. It was time for dinner.

Later, I found out there was count time at ADAPPT. Another year of living with count time. There was no escaping it.

That first night, I got a visit from Jess, the daughter of an old family friend, Lori. Lori was like a grandmother to Cain and surrogate mother to me. And Jess was like a sister.

"Jess," I cried when I saw her.

I hadn't seen any family since I'd been released. Mom promised to come visit the next day. She was working.

"Stacy, I'm so glad you're finally out!" She handed me a large cardboard box. "Merry Christmas!"

"Christmas in April?" I said with a wide smile. I opened the box. Inside were clothes, make-up, even jewelry. I closed my eyes in thankful praise.

"You're a godsend! Thank you! You might just make me feel a little more human, a little less inmate."

"Blackout's no fun," Jess said. "Since you can't leave and shop, I brought Macy's to you."

"Shoes," I squealed.

"Yeah, hope I remembered your size."

"You pegged it," I said, modeling them for her.

When she left, I called Lori. "Jess just left," I said. "She said Cain was staying with you."

"Welcome back," Lori said. "Cain's right here!"

She transferred the phone to him.

"Hi, Mommy," he said.

I took a deep breath. "I love you, baby!"

"I know," he said.

"I'm home now," I said.

"So I can come live with you, right?"

"Not yet, baby," I said. "I have to do this last little part because of what I did. Then we'll be together."

"Okay," he said. His voice became lifeless. "Okay, Mommy."

"It'll be okay, sweetie. I love you!"

It was hard to try to reassure him over the phone. He didn't cry. I didn't cry. Still, this separation was killing us both.

The next day, I went to Delores. "This isn't going to work, not with the two girls you've assigned me to bunk with."

Delores looked at me. "Why?"

"Don't make me snitch on my second day."

"Right," she said. "I'll take care of it."

I got a double room, two single beds, just one roomy. As fortune had it, she paired me with Teresa, the thin black girl I was with all through boot camp. Much better than Nelly and her friend, who probably wouldn't last long at ADAPPT. But sure as hell, I wasn't going to be the one to turn them in.

"Teresa," I said, giving her a hug. "Now that's more like it!"

She hugged me back. "Stacy Butler, I heard you were here."

"Just like old times," I said.

"But better."

We chatted through count time about everything going on at ADAPPT. Teresa filled me in on the latest gossip. Before long, Mom came. She went through the metal detector, got a visitor's pass, and sat with me. The conversation was generic, unemotional, and stiff.

Finally, I broke down. "Mom, I just want you to know that you'll never have to worry about me again," I told her. "This is the last time you'll have to deal with me on this level. I promise I'll never be the daughter I used to be."

She didn't say much, but hugged me. "Let's go."

We got in the car. I was allowed one and a half hours to do personal shopping, get things I needed. Since I had an indigent bag and Jess's care package, I asked her to take me to Effie instead. I just wanted to work.

As we drove along, I spotted an open root beer in the cup holder.

"Can I have a sip?" I asked, not taking my eye off the drink.

"Why wouldn't you?" she asked, her expression puzzled.

I shrugged. "Old habits."

It tasted good. When we got to the Charcoal Chef, I bee-lined it to Effie's office. Looking around, everything seemed the same.

Effie gave me a curt nod. "When can you start?"

I beamed. "Anytime!"

She walked away and came back with a shirt and apron. "Be here on Friday at four with your uniform."

"You can trust me, Effie."

The next day, Lori came with Cain. I was so nervous, I felt sick to my stomach. After all this time of waiting and praying to hold my son, it wasn't easy to finally hug him.

"I love you so much," I said, crushing him.

"I love you, too, Mommy," he said. "But I can't breathe."

I laughed and lightened my embrace. I couldn't bear to let him go yet. "I'm home and won't leave you again. I just can't take you yet. I have to stay here."

"What? Why?" he cried, pulling away from me.

I closed my eyes. *I have to be patient with him. He doesn't understand.*

"I have to stay here, in this place, Cain."

"When do I get to live with you?"

I forced a smile. "Soon." No point in telling him it would be a year until we'd be together again. "For now, you'll stay with Grandma and Auntie Lori, okay?"

"Okay."

I could tell it was far from okay with him. I hugged him good-bye.

The moment he left, Georgia called. "Would you like me to bring Melissa over to you at ADAPPT?" she asked.

"No," I said with a lump in my throat. "I don't want her here. ADAPPT is gross. You're not bringing her to some halfway house."

"Okay, Stacy," she said and hung up.

While I was at Quehanna, Mom had called to warn me that Georgia had left town, something she wasn't supposed to do. But who was going to stop her? Mom didn't know where she'd gone, but being the resourceful woman she was, she left a message for Georgia, letting her know she had some Christmas money for her.

Of course, Georgia called back immediately and gave Mom her address. Money rules.

What was she trying to pull now?

I dialed my Mom. She'd be able to help me sort this out.

"Mom, Georgia just called."

"What did she say?"

"She wanted to bring Melissa to ADAPPT."

Mom paused. "What did you say?"

"No."

"Smart girl," she responded.

I smiled into the receiver. "You think it was a trap, too?"

"Definitely," Mom said. "She brings your baby over and then turns around and calls your parole office, making it look like you kidnapped her."

"That thought crossed my mind."

"Don't trust her."

I paused for a moment. I felt my chest tighten. "You think she's going to try to keep my daughter?"

"Yeah, you're going to have to file for custody through the court system."

"I will. You know I will." We exchanged a few more comments, talked about Cain and then I hung up. I suppressed the tears. I ached to hold Melissa.

The next day, Thursday, was the end of blackout. I could be somewhat free, roaming around ADAPPT, going outside for a couple hours at a time. If I wanted to be out longer, I could come back and sign out again. I could stay out six hours max.

I signed out and went to a meeting for recovering addicts. Walking into the hall, I flashed back to my last time there, almost exactly three years ago, just before I went to the courthouse for sentencing. Still started at eight-fifteen on the dot. I couldn't believe that so many of the faces were the same.

The meeting began and tears started to well. I raised a shaky hand. "Hello, I'm Stacy and this is my third day home. I woke up to find there were no bars on the windows."

A murmur shot across the crowd. I heard, "Oh my God, I remember you!" from a few corners. I looked for certain people, making sure that *this* person was still there, or *that* person was okay.

One short white lady in her fifties said, "I remember the day you left. I prayed for you often, wondering how you were. I can't believe you're here! What a miracle."

"Praise Jesus," I said. "It is a miracle to be here, back at this meeting. I prayed every day to see you all again."

All my peeps came from this meeting, back before I went to prison. My sponsors, my friends, my support group, all came from this small group. That day, I met a few new people. People who knew me wanted to hug me, and people who didn't know me now wanted to.

I won't lie. I liked being the center of attention again.

Back at ADAPPT, I was still a number, going through the metal detector, signing back in. One day, maybe in a few months, if I was good and when I'd shown I could handle responsibility, I'd be allowed furloughs where I could leave for three days. It was something to look forward to.

To celebrate my new freedom, I ordered takeout Chinese with the girls. We dived into the food at one of the picnic tables set up. Forty people could eat at a time in that place, men and women.

They had standard meals that I couldn't stand. Prison food revisited. I wanted to cook for the group, but that was against the rules. So takeout was the way to go.

Looking over at a few guys playing dominos, my heart stopped when I saw a cute white guy with bright blue eyes. He was slamming down the dominoes with a few Mexican gang-member types.

After dinner, I walked up to him. "Do I know you?" I asked. "You look familiar."

He looked me up and down. "Don't know," he said with a grin. "What's your name?"

"Stacy," I answered. "Stacy Butler. And you, handsome?"

He blushed. "Jeremy Stripling."

"Hmm, Jeremy," I said, letting my eyes drop to his chest. He obviously worked out. "Maybe I had sex with you before?"

His mouth dropped. "I think I'd remember that."

"Well, it's something to consider." I tossed a look over my shoulder as I left the room. I went to bed thinking of him.

Friday was my first full day at Effie's. I wore my uniform and served my butt off. My feet and legs were shot when I got back to the halfway house. I brought home dinner from the restaurant and fell onto the picnic bench.

"You look exhausted," Jeremy said, coming up to me.

"Too tired to do much but eat," I said, looking up at him with a weak smile.

"Let me help," he said. He rubbed my shoulders as I continued to eat. I couldn't help but moan with pleasure.

He leaned down, his breath tickling my ear. "I'm glad you like it," he said. "And I can be sure we've never had sex. I'd remember your delightful pleasure noises."

I shuddered. "It's been three years,"

"I like that," he said. "It'll be like breaking your cherry again, without the pain."

When I went to bed that night, I couldn't think of anything but Jeremy's hands on my body. My dreams turned racy as I thought of ways we might meet in secret.

It was strictly taboo to enter into a relationship with someone else from ADAPPT. No fraternization. If caught, you'd be sent back to jail. Not worth it.

But a girl can dream...

Cameras were up all over ADAPPT. I was still property of the state, someone not to be trusted.

However, I couldn't help myself.

The next day, I joined Jeremy at a game of pool in the common room. We talked until six in the morning. On the weekends you could stay up as late as you like, no curfew. During the week you had to be in bed by midnight. Since the room was teeming with people, I kept my eyes low and focused on the game, only stealing glances at his body now and then.

"Good shot," he said.

"I need a good, hot shot of something hard," I muttered.

He laughed. "Are you saying you like my stick?"

I let a moan escape. "You know how to carry wood."

"Care to examine my balls?"

I looked at the table and then studied his crotch. "Nicely placed."

The banter went on and on. Slowly, the conversation turned more serious and we talked about Cain and Melissa.

Finally, about two in the morning, we were alone. I put down my stick and said, "I'd really like to have sex with you."

"Well, I don't," he replied sincerely.

I was insulted. "What?" I cried.

"No, no," he said. "Don't get me wrong. I want you. Man, do I want you, but I want to be your man, for real. I want to love you, not just fuck you."

"It's only been two days!" I said.

"I like your uniform," he said. "You know and understand work. I love that you have children and that you're a recovering addict like me."

"Look," I said. "I have no interest in having a boyfriend right now. I'm recovering, like you, just like you said. It wouldn't be right." I walked up to him and pushed him back into a corner of the room. I knew how the place was laid out. We'd be invisible to the cameras in that spot. I kissed him hard, snaking my tongue around his. "This is what I want," I murmured into his mouth, letting my hand slide down his pants to grasp his hard-on.

He pulled my hand up. "Not now, not yet."

"Then, when?"

"When you admit that you care for me, for real."

☙❧

Two weeks later, my life was turned upside down. For one thing, I fell down at work, carrying a tray of filet mignon. Effie had to pay me workman's comp. A hundred dollars a week, since I'd established two weeks of twenty-five hours a week.

I came back to ADAPPT with a cast and found Jeremy sitting in the kitchen, looking serious. "What's up?" I asked.

He pulled out a gold wedding band. "I picked this up at a pawn shop today. One day you're going to be my wife. Put it on your finger."

I slipped it onto my ring finger and smiled. "Oh my God!"

"I just want you to know that I consider you to be my wife as of now."

I looked at him. "I can't really wear this, you know."

"Yeah, I know. But one day you will."

"You're going to have to realize that you're like number four," I told him.

"Number four?" he asked with a smile.

"Yeah, because God is number one."

"That goes without saying. Who's number two?"

"Me," I said with a grin.

He chuckled. "Of course, three and four would be Melissa and Cain."

"So that actually makes you number five then," I said.

"Agreed," he said.

"One more thing," I stated.

"Anything…" he responded in a hushed tone.

"You have to get serious about your recovery. That means getting back in touch with your mom."

He thought about it for a moment before nodding. "Okay."

Had we been on the outside, we would have moved in together within two weeks. Here, we had to take our time, hide the relationship, and keep things grounded. It wasn't crazy love like I was used to, passion-filled romance with no substance. This was calm and real.

One month later, Jeremy bought me a diamond pendant shaped like a crown for my birthday. He placed it around my neck, saying, "My queen deserves to wear a crown."

Shit, someone was calling me 'queen' again.

The next month, I was released to work at Effie's again.

It was seven o'clock, during my evening shift, when I got a call from Lori. "I'm sorry to do this to you, but I can't take Cain anymore," Lori said.

"What?" I cried.

"He just went crazy and busted up one of my doors," she said. "No warning."

I closed my eyes and leaned back against the wall. *Shit, what was I going to do now?*

"I'm at work."

"I know," she said. "It just happened."

"Can you call Mom?"

"She's at work, too, so I can't reach her. Besides, I think he needs more care than either one of us can provide."

"I need time," I said.

Lori paused. "He can't stay here another night."

"Okay, give me a few hours."

"Okay."

I hung up and called Service Access Management. S.A.M. advocates for special needs children. Thank God, they had an emergency contact number.

I then dialed Delores.

"Delores, I'm at Effie's. I need to find a place for Cain to stay tonight."

"What happened?" she asked.

I explained all the details. "I might need to stay out later than curfew."

"Go to your sponsor, Alicia's, house and I'll keep tabs. Just call me regularly. You've got to let me know what's happening. Okay?"

I breathed a sigh of relief. *Thank God for Delores.* "You got it."

Effie let me go and Alicia picked me up. I didn't drive. She offered to pick up Cain, so Lori could be relieved. I needed Cain to be with me.

We called S.A.M. several times, along with other agencies, trying to find a solution in the middle of the night.

"Look, I can take him for one night," Alicia said.

"No," I said. "Thank you so much, but we have to find a permanent solution."

"But maybe it would be better to call around tomorrow."

"I really think it's got to be tonight. We have a better chance if the situation's urgent. Otherwise, it will probably drag on and on."

Finally, at one in the morning, we found Cain a home through S.A.M. It was with an African woman, who through God's grace lived a mile from ADAPPT. I dropped him off, thanking her profusely, before heading back to ADAPPT, exhausted.

When I walked in, Jeremy was up waiting. He looked like hell. His eyes had a sort of haunted look that made my heart leap in my chest.

He's really worried!

"What happened?" he asked.

"Don't worry, baby, I'm fine. Cain had an episode."

"I thought..." His voice broke. He couldn't complete the thought.

"I'm sorry, sweetie. I had no way to tell you anything."

He hugged me tight. "I'm just glad you're home."

Home. What an odd word for this place.

Jeremy took it upon himself to visit Cain every day he could. He'd walk up to the African lady's home and bond with my son.

One day, Cain broke his glasses. But, thankfully, Jeremy came up with the two hundred dollars needed to get him new glasses. He had a little bit of cash from some subcontracting and electrical work he'd landed. He didn't have much, but what he had, he gave to me and my children.

"Cain is my number one priority," was all he said.

അങ്ങ

I filed a motion to gain custody of Melissa as early as I could. I got dressed in a black wool suit and went to court with my lawyer. Butterflies danced in my stomach as I approached the room.

What did Melissa look like? Would she remember me?

The girls in prison all reassured me that my daughter would know me, instinctively. She'd feel a pull to me and I would to her. The truth was that I ached to hold my baby girl in my arms.

We were immediately informed that Georgia had cancelled. I was crushed, but managed to keep myself together. We rescheduled for the following week. Again, I dressed in the same suit, anxious and excited, only to discover that Georgia had not shown up again.

I couldn't help it. I burst into tears.

After the fourth missed hearing, I asked, "I don't know if my daughter is alive. Does Melissa Butler exist?"

"Ms. Butler," the judge said. "You should count your lucky stars that Georgia Larosh has been so generous to take care of your daughter." She pulled out a letter from opposing council. "It says here that Ms. Larosh couldn't take off time from work and doesn't have the funds to drive all the way to Reading."

She wasn't ever supposed to leave Reading!

"Yes, your honor," I said.

CHAPTER 13

Four months later, the judge finally relented. He ordered Georgia to appear before his court or suffer serious consequences. I knew she would actually come the next time.

By that time, I was working for Effie full time. I was rebuilding my life, getting more and more freedom. I could sign out for weekend furloughs from ten o'clock Saturday night, lasting forty-eight hours.

In order to leave ADAPPT at the end of my sentence, I needed to obtain a permanent residence. Sure that was still eight months away, but I'm a planner. I had to be. Having a good home was the only way I'd ever get custody of Melissa.

Jeremy was due to get out of ADAPPT in two months. If I could get him a good place now, he could get it all ready for us to move into upon my release. Plus, the judge would see it as a step in the right direction.

My sponsor, Alicia, had just accompanied her friend, Sally, to put her dog down. She was distraught and needed the company of friends, so we all went out for coffee immediately after.

"How old was she?" I asked.

"Thirteen," Sally said. "Her liver just gave out."

"I'm so sorry," I said.

"Maybe she didn't want to move to Florida," Sally said, laughing weakly. "The humidity is a killer."

"You're moving?" Alicia asked.

"Yeah, David's getting transferred. He'll be managing the rehab center in Pensacola. I have no idea how we're going to do it!"

"Why?" I said. "What's the problem?"

"We have a house here," Sally explained. "I can't afford two mortgages."

"Maybe I could help you," I said, glancing at Alicia, who nodded encouragingly. "I'm looking to rent a place."

"It's a mess," she said, not looking me in the eye.

"It can't be that bad," I said with a smile.

She shifted uncomfortably in the booth. "Well, if you want, you can come and see it."

We left the diner and headed for her home in Wyomissing Hills. It's where the blue blood money of Berks County resided, the country club elite, executive millionaires. It's the 90210 of our county.

Shit, can I really pull this off?

We pulled up to her home and it looked like a house the Brady Bunch could live in. It had to be worth a quarter of a million dollars at least. Looking around the outside, I figured she must be one of those crazy neat freaks, who thought a blade of grass out of place was a mess.

Sally pointed down the street. "Judge Owens lives three doors down in that green house with white trim."

"Wow," I said. "That's amazing."

We walked through the door and I did my best not to gasp. Did she catch my sharp intake of breath? Sally wasn't a neat freak. She was a hoarder. There was garbage piled up in corners, food stuck to furniture. Besides that, stuff took up practically every square inch of floor space, broken things mostly, moldy boxes, dirty dishes and anything else they could store away for later use.

Sally looked down at her feet. "I know, it's bad."

I lifted her chin and looked into her eyes. "I have a solution that will fix things for both of us. God has brought us together, you know. My boyfriend and I will fix this place up, live here, pay half the mortgage and utilities and help you show the home. It looks gorgeous from the outside and just needs a little tender loving care on the inside. We can get it sold for you."

Sally's eyes were brimming with tears. "Oh my God, wow! This is truly a God moment." We hugged and cried.

When I got back to ADAPPT, I told Jeremy about my new find.

"Where is this place?" he asked.

"Wyomissing Hills, if you can believe! It's a fucking mansion, Jeremy."

"No way," he responded in disbelief.

"Get used to it, baby," I said. "It's the only way I roll. Look, they want to meet you tomorrow."

"Sure!" he said.

Jeremy and I didn't have a car yet, so he walked all the way there, three and a half miles. I guess he made a good impression because Sally called Alicia the next day to ask when we could move in.

Just like that I had a key to a quarter-of-a-million-dollar home in my hands. It blew Jeremy away. He'd never had anything close to that in his life.

A few days later, I was getting ready for the next hearing. Georgia would be there with Melissa. There was no doubt, no way around it for her.

But I was assaulted by my worst fears. "What if Melissa doesn't like me?" I asked Jeremy.

He caressed my hair. "That won't happen."

"How do you know?"

"I just do. Trust me."

The next day, the courtroom was filled with dozens of people. Three of my program friends were there, too. I was in awe of the support that surrounded me.

When my little girl walked in through the giant double doors, the only word to describe the experience was magnetic. She was drawn naturally to the woman who had given birth to her, pulled to her real mother, her only mother. She knew exactly who I was. There was no denying our connection. Georgia could only watch helplessly.

Melissa walked right up to me and held out photographs for me to see. "Do you want to see these pictures?"

"Okay," I said, not wanting to overwhelm her with hugs and kisses. "Wow. Look, that's you at Grandma Meli's."

"That's right," she said.

"And I'm your mommy," I said.

"I know. You're Mommy Stacy," she said.

Georgia trained you to say that, didn't she, my angel? It doesn't matter. I can turn things around. You're my daughter.

"Come on, Mommy's got to sign some papers." I walked her out of the courtroom.

In the corridor, we did a little spin. Her little dress flaring out is a memory I'll hold dear for the rest of my life. She was my little girl and all was right again with the world.

℘℘℘

Children and Youth Services, as well as the Department of Corrections had to check out the house I rented thoroughly. It had to be right for the kids and a good set-up for Jeremy's home plan.

It didn't take us long to straighten up the place and make it presentable. It would take more time to make it the kind of home I'd like to live in, but for now, it would pass muster.

"How did you get this house again?" the DOC officer said.

"Luck," I said in my best impression of a humble person.

"No shit," she muttered. "I wish I lived in a place close to this!"

I hid my smile and changed the subject. The last thing I wanted was to have her deny the home plan out of spite.

Jeremy managed to find used little girl furniture somewhere, so Melissa had a Tinkerbell room, all matching. Cain's room had a football theme. Our room had shit, but that didn't matter. We were happy.

The judge ordered Georgia to call me every Thursday so that I could talk to my daughter. She refused. I'd call her and she wouldn't pick up the phone.

I was also supposed to get visitation once a month. The agreement was that I would pay for half the transportation and it would be an overnight visit, unsupervised. That didn't happen either.

Each time she violated the agreement, I took her to court, sometime in the middle of the month. The order would be for the first weekend of the month, Georgia wouldn't comply and by mid-month, we'd be in court again.

Since I was the property of the state and Georgia was the kind and generous Glenda, the Good Witch from the North, she wouldn't show up and everyone considered me an ungrateful bitch.

To be fair, what could the courts do? Ripping Melissa from Georgia's hands, putting her in the foster system, would have been horrible. It wasn't an option.

There was one time when she let me take Melissa, though. She wanted to go away in early January, by herself. So she called and said I could come and pick Melissa up. It was a whim.

By that time, Jeremy was out of ADAPPT, living in Wyomissing Hills, waiting for me to come join him on the weekends. We didn't take the Christmas tree down, knowing Melissa would be there. I wrapped tons of presents, put them all around the tree and waited for the day to arrive.

Renny, a lady from my meetings, offered to drive us out to get her. It was a wonderful one-hour drive back. We talked about everything a two-and-a-half-year-old is into. Barbie and My Little Pony were the hot topics.

When we arrived at the house, Melissa squealed, "Santa's been here!"

"That's right, darling," I said.

Everything was fine at the beginning, but then as I looked at her, I kept thinking about how she'd be leaving again in two days. She looked so fragile, so precious, I started to freak out. Thankfully, Renny was there for me when I suddenly burst into tears and rushed from the room. She even helped Melissa get to bed. I couldn't calm down enough to help her sleep.

My little girl is here. What the hell do I do?

The next day, tons of people came to visit and see my daughter. They all were rooting for me, the underdog. I made a turkey. Why not? After all, it was Christmas in January, wasn't it? It was way overwhelming to me, but not for Melissa. She was fine, a little princess.

That night, I pulled out *The Little Red Lighthouse*, one of my childhood favorites. Mom loved to climb into bed with us and read it when she could.

Melissa was so bright. She had many questions. "Where's the Hudson River?"

"That's just north of us, in a place called New York," I answered.

"I know New York," she said. "Mommy Georgia takes me there sometimes."

Mommy Georgia?

"That's nice," I said.

I read a little more and her eyes started to droop. As I kept reading, making my voice calm and quiet, I heard her soft snores beside me. I carefully laid the book on the nightstand and snuggled down to watch her breathe in and out, in and out.

Sleep well, my miracle baby.

I brought her back to Georgia the next day. I didn't see Georgia again until March, a month before my release, when she finally responded to a harsh letter from my attorney.

She walked into the courtroom and carefully avoided my gaze. She kept running her hands through her hair, looking around the room frantically like she had lost something. I doubt she'd slept the night before.

The judge ordered Georgia to return Melissa to me on May 1st, giving me time to get out of ADAPPT on April 20th and settle into my new home. I glanced over at Georgia throughout the judge's instruction. I would have felt sorry for her if she hadn't put me through hell over the last two years.

"Ms. Larosh would like visitation rights," Georgia's attorney said.

No fucking way.

My attorney didn't have to consult with me. "That isn't possible."

At that, Georgia snapped. "If you're going to take her away from me, take her now!"

Uh oh.

"Ma'am," the judge said. "The court appreciates all you've done for this little girl, but Ms. Butler cannot take her daughter until she is released. That won't be for another six weeks."

"I know that," Georgia said nastily. She stood up and stormed out of the room.

My arms and legs lost all feeling. Turning to the judge, I asked, "What am I supposed to do now?"

He looked at me with a hard expression. "What do you think you're supposed to do? Go out there and beg her to keep your child for you for another forty-five days."

I nodded and ran after Georgia. I found her sitting on the bench outside the courtroom, looking like a rag doll left behind.

I gritted my teeth, stifling the urge to wring her neck. "So help me, Georgia," I said, sitting next to her. I grabbed her black pant leg. "If you don't take Melissa tonight, you know you'll regret it."

Out of the corner of my eye, I saw Georgia's lawyer bounding up the stairs.

Shit!

"Did you see that? Your lawyer's running up to pay a visit to Child Youth Services!" I said.

Georgia nodded, not looking at me. "I can't pay him anymore."

"You know what he's trying to do right now, don't you?"

"Foster care. Who cares? You're taking my daughter away from me," she said.

"*My daughter*, Georgia. I'm taking *my* daughter back, just as we always agreed. I just need another month and a half." As she stared off into space, I shook her leg. "Do you know what could happen to little baby Melissa in just one night of Foster Care?"

"She'll be fine," Georgia said stubbornly.

Bullshit, you know the system.

"Your daughter could be raped tonight," I said. My gentle voice wasn't working, so I turned it up a notch. "What kind of mother are you? If you don't take her for the next month, until I can get myself out of ADAPPT, and anything happens to that little girl—" I turned back into the Queen B one last time. I had to.

Georgia used to be a prostitute and fell right into line.

When she walked back into the courtroom a few moments later, she was subdued. She looked the judge in the eye. "I'll take her until May 1st."

I left the courtroom feeling safe for the first time in a long while. Soon, I'd be out of ADAPPT, living in a gorgeous home with my two children and my amazing man.

What could possibly go wrong?

CHAPTER 14

The next weekend, I was on furlough at the house. We were watching TV, cuddling, when the phone rang at nine o'clock at night. Jeremy picked up. He was pacing as he talked to whoever was on the other end of the phone. Whatever it was, it wasn't good.

He hung up. "That was your sister. Get your clothes on! Julio just beat up your mom!"

"What?" I jumped into my jeans. "My sister got beaten up by her boyfriend?"

"No, he beat up your *mom*. We have to go *now*!"

I called Renny, as she was my reliable go-to girl, always willing to drive me anywhere. She had to call in to work to get time off.

When we got to Megan's house, Mom was all bruised up, crumpled on the sofa. I'd never seen her like that.

"Oh my God!" Megan screamed. "I can't believe he did this. Oh my *God*!"

Fortunately, Renny, being a nurse, could tend to my mother. I pulled my sister into the kitchen, forcing her to sit in a chair. I handed her a box of tissues before searching through her cabinets for a glass.

"Drink this," I said, thrusting a glass of water into her hands.

She obeyed, sputtering half of it back out through sobs. "I don't understand."

I leaned across the counter. "What happened? I thought Mom got a Protection from Abuse order on Julio."

She nodded, a fresh burst of tears streaming down. "Yeah, she got the PFA. That didn't go over real well with Julio."

"Shit."

"Yeah, he put a rock through the window this morning."

"I noticed the cardboard-tape job you did," I said. "So when the rock didn't work…"

"He waited for Mom to come home after her shift. He jumped her in the yard."

He must have had some kids casing the house for him.

I stared at her. "Why the fuck are you with that piece of shit anyway?"

Megan clenched her jaw. "You were into Black and before that Jessie, remember? It's the same thing. I am following the footsteps of my big sister, the Queen B. Wasn't that what they used to call you?"

"Am I still with Black?" I shouted. Closing my eyes, I counted to ten. "We'll discuss this later. Julio's a pile of shit. I hope you realize that now." I left the room and found Jeremy.

The storm cloud hanging over Jeremy's space created a new level of fear. I had to get him to calm down, somehow, or he'd land back in jail.

"You can't go after him," I said. "I know you want to, but you can't."

"I know," he said in a slow deliberate voice.

"It's just that—"

"I'm not going to do anything stupid," he said. "I have a family now. Things are different."

That night, we called an old friend, a tall, hulking black man who had a stash of guns. He was knocking at our door within minutes, handing Jeremy guns. "Let's set up a perimeter," he said when Jeremy opened the door. He handed him a shotgun. "Take this."

"Hey, JJ," I called out.

He gave me a curt nod in response. With JJ around, I felt like we were safe for the time being. I turned to Jeremy.

"I need to get Mom to the hospital."

"I'm going to head out to Walmart to get the locks changed after I get things set with JJ," Jeremy whispered to me. He hugged me goodbye, planting a protective kiss on my forehead.

My man!

Mom was pretty beaten up, but she was discharged from the hospital after a few hours. We found her a hotel for the night.

"I can't go back there," she said, when I had pulled the soft white comforter over her shoulders.

"I know. We'll figure something out, Mom." I leaned down and kissed her forehead. "I love you."

She closed her eyes. "I love you, too." She was out quickly. I stayed and watched her sleep for a while.

Mom ended up living at the hotel for a while. Megan joined her, so their house just sat there vacant. It was a solution, I guess.

As if that wasn't bad enough, five days later I got a call from David, the owner of the house I was renting.

"I'm back in Pennsylvania," he said.

"Really, what happened?"

"I got fired."

"No shit," I said. "Sorry to hear that."

"Yeah, it sucks. Look, Sally and I need to stay at the house with you."

"Hell no, David," I said, doing my best to keep calm. "I'm renting from you. You can't stay at the house. We have a lease."

"Stacy, you know I can put you back in jail?"

I couldn't speak. He was right. Any violation, any trouble, and I could be thrown back in jail. It was always hanging over my head. And I wasn't out of ADAPPT yet. My sentence wasn't over. Almost, but not quite.

I took a deep breath and forced a smile. He might not see it, but I always believed that a smile translates over a phone line. "Do you know that we've been helping you show the house each and every week? Jeremy and I don't have a car, so that means we need to walk around the block for three hours each time the realtor comes with buyers. We always have it ready to show."

David paused. "Yeah, I know."

"We've taken really good care of your place. Look, I only need it until May 1st. That's when I get my little girl back. My parole officer needs to go through and approve my home plan right before I move out. After that, we'll move, and you can have the place back, okay?"

He agreed and we hung up.

Two days later, he called me again, right before I was getting ready to go to Effie's for my shift. "I changed my mind. It's bullshit. The house is mine and I want to live there," he said. "I'm changing the locks right now. Get your ass over here and get your shit out of my house."

"I'll be right there," I said.

I called Effie and explained the situation. I explained the situation to Delores and signed out of ADAPPT. Renny picked me up and brought me over to Wyomissing Hills. On the way, I called my mother and Jeremy, who met me there.

When I got there, I saw David and Sally with a crew of white men, all working in the back of the house, landscaping. I was the only black girl, and to top it off, I was in my Charcoal Chef's uniform. I couldn't have been more out of place.

When I walked up to the front, Mom got out of her car. She was leaning on a cane pretty heavily.

"Mom, thanks for coming!" I hugged her tight.

"Of course," she said.

I noticed a big burly guy next to David. That guy had a reputation for trouble. He was behind quite a few very violent interventions.

Shit!

The scar on his right cheek twitched as he stared me down. If he could have started fire with his mind, I'd have been cinders. I tried not to look at him, but it was hard.

Jeremy came up to stand beside me. His sponsor was there, too. I didn't know what to do, so I started reciting passages from the big book we used in our program, a program we were all a part of, a program that promoted spirituality.

Jeremy's sponsor tried reason and logic. "Look what these two have done for you."

"You mean like landscaping?" David said, indicating his crew.

"We did a ton of stuff!" Jeremy said.

I put my hand on his shoulder. It wouldn't do any good defending ourselves. Hate was in the air.

"You mean like fucking stealing my shit?" David said. "You thought you'd get away with it, didn't you, while I was away in Florida?"

"We didn't steal anything," Jeremy said. "We fixed all kinds of things."

"Like the bench?" he said. "And where the fuck are my drums?"

Jeremy couldn't respond. He, like me, didn't want to risk an altercation with this man. We both knew that mere accusations might be enough to send us back to jail.

"Why don't you fucking go back to where you came from?" yelled one of the guys tending to the back shrubs. It was a bigoted comment directed at me, because I was black. I ignored the man.

Finally, Renny threw up her hands. "Call the police."

"What?" I asked in a stage whisper. Maybe I'd heard her wrong.

"Call the cops!"

I stared at her. "*Me* call the cops? I've never done that in my entire life. Are you kidding me? Me, Stacy Butler, call the cops?"

Pre-release pimp should call the cops?

"*Yes!*" she shouted back at me. "Call the fucking cops *now!*"

My hand shook as I dialed 911 on my phone. Wyomissing cops. They were there within five minutes. When a large, retired, white Marine stepped out in his police uniform, I cringed.

Oh my God! This is a nightmare.

David acted as if it were a race to see who could get to the officer first. "Thank God, you're here," he said.

The cop looked at him before addressing us all. "Who called me?" His voice carried across the yard. Everyone was transfixed.

I raised my hand. "I did, sir."

The black girl.

"Ma'am, I'd like to talk to you."

"Yes, sir."

"What happened?"

I took a deep breath. "Sir, this is my home. I rented it from that man." I pointed at David. "He changed the locks, so I can't get in. I have my children coming this weekend. This is illegal. I know there's a process of eviction and he isn't following it."

The officer turned to David. His voice was calm and even. "Did you change the locks?"

"Yeah, so?" David replied. "It's my house."

"Is there a lease?" The officer's eyes were locked onto David's.

"It's only month to month."

"I didn't ask you that," he said slowly. "I'm going to ask you again. Is there a lease?"

"Yes, there's a lease." David was starting to sound a little like Cain got right before he had a tantrum.

I pulled the lease out of my purse. "Sir, I have it right here."

The police officer looked over the paperwork and nodded. "It looks like it is in order. Sir, I'm going to have to ask you to give her the keys to the house." He handed me back my lease and I put it in my purse.

"I don't have them," David said.

Bullshit!

"Where are the keys, sir?"

"My wife has them."

"You need to get her over here then, sir! Now!"

David called Alicia, where Sally was hanging out.

I turned to the cop. "What happens if he doesn't produce the key?"

"He goes to jail, ma'am. You have a lease. He can't just lock you out. The law's on your side."

That's a first!

"What are my options?" David said.

The officer had the patience of a saint that day, but it was wearing thin. "Give her the keys or go to jail. Those are your options."

"Okay, what the fuck. I was stalemating. I really have the key."

"Don't you mean stalling, David?" I said.

"Whatever."

"I can't believe you just had the balls to lie to the police. What else are you lying about?" I asked.

"I want all my things out of the house," David said, ignoring me. "They've robbed me of, like, ten thousand dollars' worth of stuff. I'm not going to have them stay here with all my shit."

The police officer rolled his eyes. He turned to me and asked in a gentle voice, "When would you like them to come and get their stuff?"

I looked up and tapped my forefinger to my chin. "Hmm, I think next Tuesday would be best for me."

Everyone left and I had the house for the weekend, for my furlough. It was nice. We had a cookout the next day with a bunch of people over.

My heart stopped when the grounds crew walked up. I waited for them to say what they had to say.

"Hey, man, we're sorry," they each said.

My mouth dropped open. *Not quite what I was expecting.*

Jeremy looked at them. "What made you change your mind?"

"For one thing, David's been blackballed from our program," one of them said. "No one in Reading is interested in hearing his lies. Do you know that he was caught fucking one of his patients at the rehab center? That's why he was fired."

"No shit," I said. "I wondered what the hell had happened."

"And the fucker never paid us for the yard work we did," one of the other guys muttered.

Jeremy laughed. "Want a soda?"

"Sure," they said in unison.

The one that had been vulgar with me came up and said, "Hey, I just wanted to apologize for what I said to you, you know, personally. That was fucked up."

"Thank you," I said. "I forgive you."

Later on, the general manager of a major hockey team showed up. His whole family was rooting for me. I had met his wife at one of my meetings, right when I got out of prison. She heard me speak at a convention. I'll never forget the big-ass diamond she wore on her finger.

"You, me, Starbucks," she had told me the first day we met.

After that, we were inseparable.

※※※

We didn't end up staying at the Wyomissing Hills home through the first of the month. David and Sally called my parole officer and talked shit about me. So in the end, I didn't have a house two weeks before my release.

We spent a lot of time with Mom at the hotel. I'd sign out from ADAPPT and visit her. Megan and her kids were a few doors down, but I focused on Mom. She was always there for me, now it was my turn.

"I want you to take the house," she said to me one night.

"What? No," I said. "Look, I need a place, but that's your home."

"I'm not going back to that house," she said with a firm shake of her head.

Jeremy took her hand. "You might feel differently in a few weeks."

"No, I won't. I'm scared to death to live there. I feel—" She paused and looked down. "—violated."

"I'm so sorry," I said, coming around to the other side. I rested my head against her shoulder. "Thank you for always taking care of me."

We spent the next few days putting Mom's stuff in storage. The parole officer came for a visit. I led him to the kitchen table, one of the only things we had in the house. It could have been a disaster, but in the end, it was a beautiful come-to-Jesus meeting, talking straight about everything that had gone down.

"Being honest, I came here to deny this home plan," he said. "I heard an earful from your prior landlord. Shit, can that man talk! But now, after hearing what you had to say, I'm approving you two to stay here."

So, we had two weeks to get Mom's home in order. We didn't have furniture, but so many people from the program came in to help out. One family brought a couch, another a chair and pretty soon we had a good starter set.

One of my regulars at Effie's was looking at an ad in the Auto Trader. I looked over her shoulder and said, "Oh, you're looking for a car? I'm looking for one, too."

"No," she said. "We have an old Saturn to sell. It's only $900."

"That would be a dream!"

I knew her and her husband pretty well and trusted them. They had a full inspection and it was in good shape. Mom agreed to pay for it, so I finally had a car and a house, a home.

God's amazing work!

༺༻

A month later, Mom called to tell me her best friend had died. Ariel had been sick for weeks with a rare form of diabetes. There was no cure. Her friends, a flock of white women with black husbands, all rallied around her bedside.

"Was Sierra at the hospital?" I asked.

"Yes, she was," Mom replied.

"Were you nice to her?"

"Yeah. I might even start going out to lunch with her again."

Mom had a falling out with Sierra when I took her into a bathroom one night to do lines of coke. I did it to have that sense of power over my mother's friend. It was very Queen B. When Mom found out, she had a fit.

"Would you like me to do lines in the bathroom with one of your friends?" she had asked me.

She was right, of course.

"I'm so glad you two could patch things up," I told her. "You know, when I got clean and sober, I thought I was better than all the other addicts that were using. You know, because I was sober and all. But then, after jail and ADAPPT, I realized we're all the same. We all have struggles. I'm not better than anyone. I'm just lucky. I got a chance."

"You are lucky," she said. "I'm glad you realized that."

She wasn't one to give me accolades. She just stressed that I was doing what I was supposed to be doing, like I might stop if she praised me too much.

We talked for something like ninety minutes about everything from her friends to my childhood, our family, and jail. I must have told her that I loved her a dozen times in that call.

"You know, I never told you, but when you were in jail, I was petrified," she whispered at one point.

"I'm sorry, Mom," I said. "I'm sorry I did that to you."

"My biggest nightmare was that there would be a fire and you wouldn't be able to get out. That you would be stuck in there, burned alive."

"Thank you for telling me," I told her. It was the first time she ever mentioned anything about how she felt about my being incarcerated.

When I hung up the phone, I hugged Jeremy tight. Everything was fitting into place. I'd overcome what seemed like impossible odds to achieve the American dream. I had a beautiful home, a wonderful man, two amazing children and peace with my mother.

Thank you, God!

CHAPTER 15

Everything was white, my dress, the linens, the tables, the chairs. All picture-perfect snow white. There were hundreds of party guests, all toasting me, holding up crystal flutes of sparkling cider. Even Jeremy was in white, which was strange, because I always pictured him in a black tux at our wedding.

A cell phone rang.

Who the fuck brought a cell phone to my wedding?

It took me a moment, but I recognized the ring tone. It was my mother. I began to wake up from my dream.

What? Why is she calling me now? She's right there in front of me.

The vision faded as the ringing persisted. I pulled the pillow over my head to drown out the noise, but it wouldn't stop.

"Hello?" Jeremy could never ignore a phone. "Mom! Mom!"

"Stop it," I whined. "Quit kidding around. Go back to sleep."

"Mom, where are you?" There was something about his voice, something I had never heard before. Fear!

I bolted upright and grabbed the phone. "Mom, what's going on?"

She screamed and hung up. I redialed, but no one answered.

"What happened?"

Jeremy had dialed 911 on his phone. "I'd like to report an accident on 422 somewhere between Reading and Wernersville State Hospital."

I gasped. "No!" I cried.

Jeremy hung up and said, "She'll be okay, she'll pull out of this. Stay calm."

I called all our friends on the way to the hospital. Lori stayed with the kids. When we arrived, we found out Megan had been in the car with her. For some reason Mom had stepped on the accelerator instead of the brake when she was parking and had crashed into the hospital building.

Two weeks prior, she had purchased a new home. Mom had just retired last month, so this morning she had been on her way to begin a big road trip to New York with her friends from the hospital. It was a much needed vacation for her.

When I'd learned about the trip, I wanted to go, but Mom was adamant that she was only taking Megan.

"Why?" I'd asked.

She had put a gentle hand on my shoulder. "You have a family now. You should be taking trips with Jeremy, not your old mom."

"But...Mom!"

"I have something nice planned for your birthday. Don't worry."

We went to see Megan first in the emergency trauma unit.

She saw me and started chanting, "Where are the purses? Where's Mom's purse? Where's my purse?"

I couldn't calm her down. Finally, the doctors found me and took me aside.

"Your mother's going into surgery now. She has two broken legs and a lot of internal bleeding." He left and I signed all the releases with a staff member.

Delores was there with me. "Everything's going to be okay."

Like hell it is!

Jeremy arrived, from parking the car, soon after and we waited. In a few hours, a doctor came, accompanied by a man in street clothes.

"I'm a pastor," he told me.

That can't be good!

The doctor touched my sleeve. "We opened your mother up. She's bleeding extensively. You need to come upstairs right away."

On the way up, Jeremy leaned in and whispered, "This is good. They wouldn't let us come up if it wasn't good, right?"

"Jeremy, this isn't good. The pastor's here. They don't call him in when it's good news."

The walk seemed to take forever. When I walked into the ICU trauma unit, I felt them behind me. I knew the minute I turned around they would say, "Your mom's going to die."

Just don't turn around and everything will be okay.

I knew my life was about to change. I took a deep breath and faced the doctor.

"Ms. Butler, I just want to prepare you," he said. "We've already lost your mother twice. She's on a ventilator and can't breathe on her own. We could go in and give her a procedure that would stop the bleeding, but she could have a stroke."

I looked into his hazel eyes. "What would you do if this were your mother?"

"I'd do it in a heartbeat."

"Then do it! Can I see her?"

He shook his head slowly. "That's really not a good idea. There's blood everywhere. And she might flat line again."

"If that were me in the bed, you know she'd be by my side. I have to go in there."

Fifteen doctors and nurses were in the small room. All I could do was watch helplessly from behind the glass.

"Would you like to pray?" the pastor asked.

"Yes, Father." He led us in a small prayer, holding my hand. I continued to watch the staff work on her. When she seemed to stabilize, I called Effie and Renny. They were all praying.

"I'll be right over," Renny said. True to her word, she was there in moments.

Renny was a godsend. Being a nurse, she could give me the blow by blows about what was going on. She talked to the other nurses and looked bleak.

"Call whomever you need to call," she whispered to me. "It isn't looking good."

I called my aunt and uncle and one of Mom's old friends. She then called all the women who had been at Ariel's vigil. Within thirty minutes, there were two dozen friends of my mother in that tight space. Renny stood by my side.

"We're going to make her comfortable," the doctor told me. "That's all we can do."

"Can you release my sister, so she can be here?"

"Sure," the doctor said.

When Megan came in, I had to tell her the bad news. She collapsed into someone's arms and cried.

I went into Mom's room. I leaned down and whispered, "Mom, if you want to go, you go. I'll handle everything. I'll take care of Megan. I won't get high and won't go back to jail. If you want to stay, I will take care of you the way you'd take care of me." I spoke the way she always talked to me. Plainly, the way it was.

People kept walking into that small room, friends from the hospital, street friends, and mutual friends of Ariel, they were all there. Ariel's friends were a wreck, having just lost her the day before.

The pastor offered to say a prayer.

"Thank you, Father, but I'd like Uncle Frank to do it."

Frank did a great job, said a beautiful prayer, read the twenty-third Psalm, and said three amens. After the amens, it seemed like it was over. Mom passed soon after.

೧೨೮೨

I gave a eulogy for my mother that made everyone cry. My sister couldn't form the words to express her grief, so I spoke for both of us. I didn't bury my mother as the Queen B, but rather as Stacy Butler, the daughter my mother always wanted.

Torn between a grief I couldn't seem to feel and pride that my mother saw me clean and sober before she passed, I started planning a wedding I knew she wanted me to have. She loved Jeremy and wanted us to be together. Now, with my inheritance from her, we could finally afford a wedding of my dreams.

No one proposed to anyone, it was just a logical decision. It was good to be able to focus on something other than her death, so I shifted gears and set the wedding date.

November 11, 2011. Eleven, eleven, eleven. That gave me three months to plan a wedding for two hundred guests.

I had a lot of help. Everyone was chipping in to make it happen. Visiting my friend, Ava, in Chicago, I asked her to help me pick out bridesmaid dresses.

"I need something off the rack," I told her.

"You'll love this little shop I know," she said, pulling me into the store.

When I walked in, my eyes were immediately drawn to a beautiful Vera Wang gown in the center of the store. It had its own pedestal and looked as if it were designed for a queen.

"Does that one come in plus sizes?" I asked without thinking.

"Sure," the sales lady said.

"Never mind." I shook myself. "I could never afford that."

The sales lady ignored me and brought one out in my size. It was two thousand dollars. I couldn't help myself. I put it on, along with the headpiece. It was my dress. I nodded and everyone in the store erupted into a deafening applause. I did a slow spin for my mother to see, feeling her presence.

As the day approached, everything went smoothly and I lost myself in the preparations. I was on a pink cloud of pre-marital bliss. Jeremy took over on all other aspects of our lives, giving me space to grieve and plan our big day.

Jeremy and I were madly in love. We couldn't stop touching each other, kissing, making love. My uncle, who would officiate our wedding, wanted us to stay apart for the week before the wedding, but there was no way. We didn't even pretend to consider that option.

Predictably, my sister was full of resentment, grief, and anger. She was a mess at the rehearsal dinner, doing her best to sabotage everything. She showed up drunk and insulted my singer over and over. Fortunately, my friends ran interference and the singer brushed it off like a professional.

Later, after the dinner, my sister gave me a pendant of my mother's as a wedding gift. It would have been touching had the piece not actually been willed to me. I didn't want to fight with her over it, so I just thanked her.

The next morning, Megan continued her nasty games, announcing that she and her family weren't coming to the wedding. Since they were all in the wedding party, I was devastated.

"Don't worry about it," Ava said, putting an arm around my shoulder. "Just leave her alone. It isn't worth it."

I nodded, but realized that I couldn't let it go. Mostly because I knew my sister would regret it later. I was only getting married once and she just had to be a part of it. In the end, she changed her mind and came.

The wedding and dinner went off without a hitch. Pink Gerber daisies lined the eighty-foot aisle of the Spring Valley Church of God. They were off-season, so my florist had them flown in. He stayed through the wedding, so that he could bring them all to the reception for me.

My sister fell into line during the ceremony. When she took my bouquet from me, I took it as a sign of peace.

Walking into my reception hall, Canal Street's backroom, I was entranced. The room had many windows looking out to the woods. There was an artsy old-time flare to the place, a peaceful setting. It was kind of funny having a dry reception at a pub, but the staff understood and everyone was supportive.

Each table had its own pumpkin cake with white frosting as a center piece, appropriate for the time of year. Cain and Melissa were there for part of the reception, but after the dinner was over, Renny took them home. She and other friends offered to watch them while Jeremy and I were honeymooning in Miami.

We made it to the airport with plenty of time to spare. On the plane, the stewardesses announced, "We have newlyweds on the plane!" Everyone clapped and they handed us a huge magnum of champagne. We thanked them and promptly handed the huge bottle to two ladies sitting near us on the plane, who were grateful for the gift.

When we got to the Trump International, our room was immediately upgraded to a double suite on the nineteenth floor. It was extravagant with a marble bathroom, complete with a separate shower and tub. We even had two balconies.

We spent the first day just walking along the beach and dining in our room. We made excellent use of the butler, who served us on silver platters in our private dining room. Neither of us had ever experienced such luxury before.

The next morning, we went to see the Miami Dolphins. I had bought fifty-yard line seats, which was pretty good, but when I got there, I realized I could have done better.

"I wish I'd gotten field seats," I murmured.

"Hungry?" Jeremy asked.

"I could eat."

"Give me a second."

He was gone for twenty minutes before my cell rang. "Yes, my husband?"

"You've got to come down here," he said. "I'm at the bottom of the steps."

I found him talking to a large black woman wearing a blue shirt. She gave me a huge smile.

"And this must be the new Mrs. Stripling!" She put a wristband on me and called over two staff members. "Escort these newlyweds from Pennsylvania to their new seats in the VIP section."

We were featured on the megatron and had our pictures taken with the cheerleaders. The Queen B would have felt like she deserved all this. That wasn't me. I was now a clean and sober Mrs. Stripling, perhaps with a touch of royalty.

Jeremy and I met up with Renny's parents, who were retirees. Her mom worked for Coach, so I got some killer discounts. I ended up purchasing four handbags.

It's my honeymoon. Why not splurge?

We ate out every night at five-star restaurants and hit the casinos after. Money wasn't a consideration. However, we were in bed by nine.

To celebrate our wedding, Jeremy and I both got matching cross tattoos with "11/11/11" and "Stripling" across them. I also decided to finally augment my Queen B ink to read "Missi B," in honor of my mother and daughter bearing the same name. Mom would have loved it. She never liked the Queen B.

The night before we left, reality hit. I had gotten used to living like royalty and wasn't ready to return to the real world. The pink cloud had vaporized. I'd spent a small fortune from the money Mom had left me. It had created a temporary happiness, which was now quickly coming to an end. Things started to crash in on me.

We got home and fell into a routine. Thanksgiving rolled around and Missy was released from prison. I invited her and her son to move in with us on a temporary basis. Being able to help a good friend perked me up.

I could also make financial amends with various friends. I enjoyed tracking down all the people who had given me money, even small loans of gas. I finally had the money to pay people back, giving them what they needed.

Not everyone was grateful. Some of my friends had disappeared. I could imagine that they probably resented me and my newly found wealth. I could finally afford nice cars, good clothes and I wasn't stressed about money.

I was grateful to my mother for allowing me to experience the finer things in life while being clean and sober. However, I still wasn't really grieving, but just holding everything in. I wasn't facing what was really going on.

I remember a time at ADAPPT when I ran into a man sitting in the kitchen eating a chicken salad. I sat down across from him and smiled.

"You're making that salad look like it cost a thousand dollars."

"Well to me, it is," he said. "I was in jail for ten years. I wanted this salad for ten years."

Two weeks later, he was on restriction for some minor infraction. I couldn't believe it. Who would risk going back to jail?

"Yo, do you remember the day I watched you eat that salad?" I asked him. "You remember that day?"

His blank look changed into one of dawning recollection before my eyes. "I'd forgotten," he breathed.

"You can't forget," I told him. "You just can't. You gotta remember that salad for the rest of your life."

Just like I have to remember being chained to that bed when I was having my baby.

I continued to spend Mom's money like there was no limit. We had three trees that Christmas and way too many presents. New Years came and went and Jeremy and I settled into a new routine, where he'd take care of everything and I would stay in bed.

Jeremy would get up at six in the morning and have breakfast with the kids, getting Cain off to school. Then he'd take Melissa out all morning. I'd sleep through all that, waking up at noon. That's when I'd call him.

"It's time for you to come back," I'd tell him.

"I'll be right there. What do you need?"

I'd place my lunch order with him and he'd bring it home and serve me. I never thanked him. In my mind, he was just doing what he should. I mean after all, my mother's money was paying all the bills. It was the least he could do.

Jeremy was getting more and more on my nerves. The laundry was never folded right, the house wasn't in perfect order and I just knew my gut-wrenching misery had something to do with his inadequacies.

"You're lucky you can do one thing right!" I'd tell him snidely over and over on a regular basis. We still had sex a few times a week. He'd ignore all my digs and just keep silent.

One day, Melissa told me about some new friends they'd met at the park. My heart skipped a beat.

"What new friends?" I asked her.

She named a few women and I immediately confronted Jeremy. "Who are these girls?"

He didn't look me in the eye. "Just some girls we met."

"You're cheating on me."

"No way."

"Liar."

I started hating it when he'd leave the house. I knew where he was going and knew I was pushing him away, into the arms of another girl, but I couldn't help myself. He was cheating on me and it hurt. I blamed him for all my misery.

Finally, he couldn't take it anymore. "I'm moving in with my mother." He took a few suitcases and boxes of stuff. Later, on Easter Sunday, he returned for the rest of his stuff.

I followed him into the bedroom. "I need to know the truth."

"What are you talking about?"

"The girl."

"I told you—"

"Look, Jeremy," I cut him off, "if you want to take my daughter out, I need to know where she's going. Just tell me, who is she?"

He stopped moving around the room and sat on the edge of the bed. "Yanamaria."

"The cute Spanish girl at the pharmacy?"

"That's right. She has a daughter. She gets me."

When he left, I decided it was a good time to pick up my meds. I found her behind the counter.

"Can I help you?" she asked with a big smile.

"Yes, you can. My name is Stacy Butler Stripling. Nice to meet you," I said, piercing her brown eyes with mine.

Her smile vanished. I shook her hand and felt her tremble.

I ordered the meds and signed "Stripling" really big on the screen. She got the message.

Six weeks went by and I filed the paperwork for a divorce. I blocked Jeremy's number on my phone. I was done with him. I hooked up with a friend of a friend. Jeremy had left the downstairs and living room half-painted, so my friend brought over a young stud, Justin, to finish the job. He was just my type. I think my friend intended for this boy, and he was just a boy, to be more like entertainment for me, but I took him in.

I posted pictures of Justin up on Facebook, knowing that Jeremy would see. He retaliated by posting pictures of Yanamaria. I checked his page a few times a day, so I caught the posting showing off his latest gift to her, a Cadillac purse.

He's buying his girlfriend a purse to match my car.

I still went to Yanamaria's pharmacy. I mean, why shouldn't I? As luck would have it, he was there one day when I showed up. I put my Coach purse on the counter.

"FYI," I said loudly. "Your boyfriend, my husband, bought me this purse in Miami. It's a Coach, very classy. The Cadillac bag, not so much."

The girl had a sense of humor. She laughed.

I walked by Jeremy. "High five to the wife."

He chuckled and obliged. It was one of those exits I couldn't have planned better.

By the end of the summer, Cain started telling me, "Dad will be home soon."

"What makes you say that?" I asked.

"Football season is about to start."

"So?"

"There's no way he's not coming home for football season." For Cain, Daddy and football were synonymous.

Unfortunately, my new boyfriend liked to drink. I stayed sober, but allowed him to drink in the house, which went against everything I believed in. It went against my program, so my solution was to stop going. I didn't want any lectures. I liked Justin, maybe a little too much. He made me feel like a teenager again.

My friends were pissed at me, but the friend that had introduced us was really ticked off.

"He wasn't supposed to be more than a good lay, Stacy!" he told me.

"I like him."

Justin's drinking got worse and we'd get into stupid fights, giving us a reason for great make-up sex. One night, we got into a scuffle over my phone. The phone slid under my bed as we both reached for it.

"If you've nothing to hide, give me your fucking phone," he said.

"You're way out of line," I shouted.

"You're cheating on me, you fucking bitch," he yelled, so loud the neighbors could hear.

"You're crazy in the head!"

"Do you think you're the fucking Queen B? You're not, you know. If you were the fucking Queen B, your husband wouldn't have left you!"

We continued to scream at each other, but his words hit home. Justin was right. I didn't want to be the Queen B. That was an old chapter.

I miss Jeremy.

Ten minutes later, there was a knock on the door. Cain opened the door and allowed two police officers in. Justin went off on them, spouting every obscenity known to man. Being that he was on probation for a DUI and was drunk as a skunk, they hauled him away.

It was time for him to go. Things were adding up in one direction. It was clear to me that I had made a huge mistake. I unblocked Jeremy's number and left a message for my lawyer, cancelling the divorce process. I didn't want to wait for the morning.

As it turned out, the receptionist called me first thing. "I got your message. Are you sure, Mrs. Stripling?"

"Yes, I'm sure."

"You know that Mr. Stripling is due to come in at eleven, right?"

"No, I didn't know that," I said. "Please cancel the meeting."

Early afternoon, I got a text from Yanamaria's phone. *This is Jeremy. I'm texting from this phone, because you blocked my phone. What's happened with the lawyer and the divorce?*

I texted, *NO DIVORCE.*

He didn't text back. I didn't want to say too much through Yanamaria, so I emailed him. *I will always be your wife in God's eyes.*

I didn't hear back and wondered if he might be embarrassed to come back. Maybe he didn't realize I wanted him. I needed to be more direct.

The next day, I sent another email. *No matter what happens, you're always welcome here. This is your home. You are my husband and the father to my children.*

I didn't think I could be clearer.

The next day, Renny came over and handed me a bouquet of pink Gerber daisies. "I'm supposed to bring you these," she said with a wide grin.

"Who are they from?"

"Who do you think?"

Later, he emailed me. *I know I made a lot of mistakes. I left you when you needed me the most. Can I call you later?*

I wrote back one word. *YES!*

He called the house phone. "I want to come home."

That was all I wanted to hear. "When are you coming?" I asked.

"How about now?" he said.

Thank you, Lord! I am truly blessed.

END

About the Author

Stacy Butler is a novice author with a huge story to tell. Her new book, *They Called Me Queen B* reflects the true story of her life. Butler was born and raised in Reading, Pa. A homecoming queen, cheerleading star, and softball champion, she turned to the dark side and into the infamous Queen B who dealt drugs with kingpins, pimping penthouse pets, and finally ending up doing 4-8 years in the state penitentiary. Her story, however graphic, is one of recovery and inspiration. Butler is now married, living with her husband and her children, and has been sober for 8 years.

Made in the USA
Middletown, DE
02 August 2021